It Is Written

A JOURNEY TO DISCOVERING THE FATHER

ADRIA KING

WESTBOW
PRESS®
A DIVISION OF THOMAS NELSON
& ZONDERVAN

WestBow Press books may be ordered through booksellers or by contacting:

WestBow Press
A Division of Thomas Nelson & Zondervan
1663 Liberty Drive
Bloomington, IN 47403
www.westbowpress.com
1 (866) 928-1240

Unless marked otherwise, all Scripture quotations are taken from The Holy
Bible, English Standard Version® (ESV®), Copyright © 2001 by Crossway,
a publishing ministry of Good News Publishers. All rights reserved.

Scripture quotations marked NIV are taken from The Holy Bible, New
International Version®, NIV® Copyright © 1973, 1978, 1984, 2011 by
Biblica, Inc.® Used by permission. All rights reserved worldwide.

ISBN: 978-1-9736-8345-2 (sc)
ISBN: 978-1-9736-8344-5 (hc)
ISBN: 978-1-9736-8346-9 (e)

Library of Congress Control Number: 2020900457

Print information available on the last page.

WestBow Press rev. date: 1/14/2020

Contents

February 4, 2014

Dear Halle,

I dedicate this to you. Throughout the pages of this book, I pray that my voice is silenced. I pray that Jesus speaks and makes it so clear to you that you are not fatherless. May we journey together far beyond these pages.

Introduction

"Tell me your story." You've heard it said. Maybe you have been the one to say it, or maybe you have been on the other end of things, and it has been asked of you. We sit around campfires and share testimonies. Am I the only one who has ever noticed that as the night goes on, the stories just seem to get more and more intense? Sometimes we alter our stories. There comes this need for our brokenness to one-up someone else's.

I have been asked to share my story more times than I can even count, and if I am honest, this phrase has wounded me a little bit. I want to make sure we are clear in what we want from people when we use this phrase because the meaning of it can get lost in translation. We don't want to leave people feeling like they have a nametag on themselves. We don't want them to feel like they're labeled with that one specific part of their life that they probably think we are referring to when we ask for their story.

That's how I felt. Scratch that, it is still how I feel sometimes. The moment the words come out of someone's mouth is the same moment my mind asks this question: *Do they want to know about my dad*? This might not always be the intention. However, somewhere along the way, this is what my reaction came to be. I want to retrace my steps to see when I got the cords twisted because storytelling is not an ineffective thing, nor is it a bad thing. We have to do it right, though.

Jesus was a storyteller. I believe He spoke in parables because He knew the simplicity of stories was something that our finite minds could understand. His stories weren't long. Often times

He was a man of few but meaningful words. Imagine the tone of voice He probably chose when speaking. We read Scripture like it is a Shakespearean play, but it wasn't. Jesus' voice was kind. He didn't yell. He drew you in. He calmed you. He told us that He is rest. I imagine it would have been impossible to leave listening to Jesus and feel more exhausted. Have you ever left after listening to someone talk and felt more emotionally exhausted than when you got there?

When I think of stories, I think of being a little girl getting ready for bed. I see myself running to the bookshelf in the corner of my room and getting to pick out just one book for my mom to read to me before I fell asleep. I think about the many nights I babysat. I would tuck the children in, and they would climb up into the bed next to me with as many books as their arms could carry. I think of all the movies I have seen where a kid would ask either a parent or a grandparent to tell them a story. There was something about not picking the book, something about what was coming being a surprise, and it always being different than the one you heard the night before.

But, we all had the favorite book, the one we had read a million times but still persistently asked to have it read again. If the storyteller told the story the right way, there was never a moment where we would grow tired of hearing the same narrative.

Don't hear me say that telling your story more than once, to different people, or even telling it over and over again is a bad thing. Do hear me say that there is a right way to do it and a wrong way to do it. We have lost the art of storytelling because we are tempted to start camping out on one page and never letting people in on the before and after. We are tempted to do this because we believe the lie that all we have to offer is the tragic climax. You'll come to see that what people really want when they hear a story is the evidence of hope. You can create that without feeling the need to give an in-depth, drawn-out, long-winded account. Hope is Jesus. If you talk clearly about what He has done, then there will be more hope coming from your lips than there is anything else.

Stories weren't meant to be repetitive. Stories weren't meant to stay on the same page. Stories were meant to be simple, not over emotionalized. Stories were meant to have a main character, and it's not us. Sadly, our stories have become so self-focused.

If I am sharing my story with someone and they walk away knowing only about me, then I have failed. They need to walk away knowing all about my Jesus. The best stories are the ones with unexpected endings. That is why we can't just share the "thing" we think everyone wants to know about—your eating disorder, your addictions, your struggles with self-harm, your parents' divorce, etc. Don't ever deny the existence of the reality of these things in your life. But know that there is more to you than just what you have been through. We can't only share where we were; we have to share where we are now.

Stories have chapters. We give people whiplash if we skip right to the "bad" and don't let there be any context for what led up to these moments we are sharing about. We are leaving the things out that God has clearly written into the story if we let the "before" go unsaid. It is not giving credit where credit is due. Peel back the layers slowly. No one told us that we had to lay it all out there for every single person we come in contact with. Coffee dates do not have to be memoirs shared verbally.

One summer, I was having a conversation with a friend about this very idea. I was working at a camp as the speaker for middle school and high school-aged girls. At camp, every Monday was the day I shared a little bit about losing my dad. As the summer progressed, I genuinely wasn't in a good place with it, and to share it was causing emotional turmoil that was not a healthy place to teach from. I kept explaining to my friend that I didn't have a backup plan, though.

What else was I going to talk about?

She kindly, yet firmly reminded me, "That is not the only time in your life that you faced a hard time. You are still letting yourself think that it is all you have to offer."

I didn't talk about my dad from stage anymore that summer.

Not because what God has done through that is not evident and worth talking about, but because it was what my heart needed. You can be protective of your story. Notice I said protective, not selfish. Always guard your heart in those moments. Pull back when you need to. Don't let yourself believe that to not share something is going to take away from the potential of what God is going to do. Sometimes to not share is just as powerful as to share. He promises that His word will not return void. Use more of His words, less of your own. The potential for what could happen automatically increases.

We have over complicated storytelling. Paul puts it this way when writing to the church at Corinth: "We are afflicted in every way, but not crushed; perplexed, but not driven to despair; persecuted, but not forsaken; struck down, but not destroyed" (2 Corinthians 4:8-9)

We are _____, but not _____

Paul said, yes, we are afflicted, but we aren't crushed. We are struck down but not destroyed. It was the confession of the struggle paired beautifully together with the reminder of the hope. I don't walk away from Paul's words thinking only about what he was going through. I leave thinking about what God was doing in the middle of it. We need both. People need both. It is doable.

We can individualize the layout Paul used.

I am _____, but not _____

To do away with the phrase, "Tell me your story," won't happen, but I think as people of the church, we can make sure that we don't throw the phrase around like confetti. We can make sure that people know our hearts behind our curiosity. We can make sure that they know when we say the word *story* we don't just mean that one page.

I want people to know that I want to know them, not just their story. Because when that question gets asked, the odds are there are a lot of people out there, like me, who instantly leave out so much. I want to know people, not just stories. There is too much of a risk to only know characters if we just know stories. Sometimes people get lost in the story, but people matter the most. I don't want you to know my story; I want you to know me. I want you to know that behind all these words, there is a real person who is really no different than you. I want you to know the real me, not just the select couple pages of me that I seem to have memorized a script for and gotten really good at sharing.

Most importantly, we can share our story, but we have to share His story more.

This book—it's the whole story. It's the before, the messy middle, the here and now, and a look into what's to come. Really, we all have the same story when we are followers of Jesus; there are just personal versions of it. Here's mine. It goes a little something like this:

I am still figuring out how to navigate life without an earthly father, but I am finding everything I thought I lost is found in Jesus.

Yellow Gatorade

It was snowing outside. The driveway wasn't in a state where you could drive on it, but somehow Dad managed to back out of it and make his way to the front of the neighborhood. We were the first house on the left. It didn't take long before you reached the main road and had to decide which way to turn. If you were to take a left, you were headed toward the local schools. We usually always took a left, as every morning we headed down the road we lived on to our elementary school. If you were to take a right, it usually meant you were headed to the interstate, the possibilities endless.

I was seven. I was barely tall enough to see out one of the side windows on our front door. Back then, I thought I was a little taller, a little older, and a little smarter than I really was. Somehow I stood tall enough that day. I had my snow boots on, so it gave me a little extra lift. My ringlet, curly hair was pulled into a ponytail. I dripped water everywhere after I had sat in front of our fire and started to defrost from being outside all morning.

Dad turned right that morning. I didn't know where he was headed. I hoped he was going to the store to buy some snow day snacks. You would think this was an all too normal day. However, when I walked away from that smudgy window, where I had smashed my nose into it far too many times to count, normal was the farthest thing from what I was entering into.

My dad went to a doctor's appointment that day, the first of many. I don't know the exact moment my parents sat me down and tried to explain to me that my dad had been diagnosed with diabetes, but it happened at some point. When I imagine myself as a seven-year-old hearing the word "diabetes," I am sure that I thought nothing of it. I mean, come on people, I wasn't far past the day where I was given the tragic news that Santa wasn't real.

People ask me all the time if I remember when my parents told me, "Daddy is sick." Part of me thinks that somewhere underneath the feelings, I have pushed down that memory. It is there, but today, it doesn't come to mind. That time of my childhood is fogged, blurry. There are few recollections of what those days looked like. I am always left wondering, "Do I remember this?" or "Do I just know this because I have heard it countless times?" Deciphering the two might be unobtainable.

I know that at some point, diabetes turned into stage four pancreatic cancer. I know that Dad started to lose weight. The pictures I have from that time prove that to be true. He was grumpy at times. I am sure I would have been too. I can still see as clear as day him coming around the corner that had my parents' bedroom tucked into the back and his body frame making me feel numb. He was skin and bones; it was nauseating to look at. They tell you what the cancer is, but they don't tell you what cancer looks like. I knew, even at that age, that I didn't like the way it looked.

Dad went to the hospital a lot. We basically lived there. Yet, I still thought nothing of the extremity of this. When you are sick, that meant mom was going to give you some yellow Gatorade and saltine crackers, and then you would be better. Who needed medicine when you had yellow Gatorade? That stuff is a miracle worker. Am I right?

Mom started to be gone a lot, and Dad, well, he stopped coming to school to read books to my class. You see that's what my dad did. In his fancy work clothes, he would leave his office, where he sold insurance, and drive the half-mile from his office to my elementary school. He would walk down to my first-grade class, where you could find him probably reading "The Three Javelinas." I think as children, we don't really understand something is wrong until what is expected and normal stops happening. When my dad stopped coming to read to my first-grade class, I knew something was wrong, but I didn't fully understand.

People started showing up at our door night after night with food and uncomfortable smiles. Why is it that people think the only thing to do when someone is sick is to deliver food? I wanted someone to take me to the playground, not bring another casserole. I wanted something normal. Yet for some reason, that is all people know to do. People I did not even know delivered a knock on the door and a tinfoil wrapped pan, accompanied by a demeanor that tried to hide that they didn't know the plot unfolding in our household. They all knew what I didn't.

At age seven, the word cancer doesn't have the sting it does now that I am in my twenties and know the weight and the territory that terrifying word comes with. I am thankful that in my complete childlikeness, fear had no place. However, I didn't need to have a total sense of awareness to know that my dad wasn't getting better, in fact, he was only getting worse.

In our living room, there is an entertainment center that has a lot of drawers. Some hold old VHS movies. Some hold all of our games, missing pieces and all. In one of those drawers, you can find multiples of the game Scattergories. It is my family's favorite. Yet for some reason, we can never keep up with where we had it last. Instead of looking for it, we buy another copy.

One drawer is a drawer of miscellaneous items that includes this one particular picture that I love. The picture isn't framed, and it rarely makes its way out into public, but I know it is there. There is nothing special about the place the picture was taken, but the people in it make it special. There are men and women of all ages, on a golf course, with a sign that still hangs in our basement. That sign reads: Greg King Golf Tournament.

My dad was running out of options. There were rumors of

treatment variations that they did in Mexico that were different than those in the states. They thought it might help him. Our family and friends linked brains and came up with the idea to host a golf tournament where all the proceeds would go to my dad's trip to Mexico.

Chick-fil-A biscuits for breakfast, Mo-Joe's chicken wings for lunch, followed by an auction at the end of the night with a TV that I am still mad we didn't win. They raised enough money that day and more for my dad to be able to go to Mexico. My mom, my aunt, my uncle, and my dad packed their bags, and off they went.

The thing about that picture that sits in that drawer is that every now and then, I will pull it out and notice a person I didn't see before. Someone that I have come to know in a more significant way over the years.

"Mom, did you know Coach Sam played in that golf tournament for Dad?" I asked her.

Coach Sam was one of my friend's dads. He took me to more softball and volleyball tournaments than I can count. He bought me more meals after practice than I will ever be able to pay him back for. To this day, he tells me stories about my dad that make my heart smile. It was years after the golf tournament took place, and even years after I met Coach Sam that I realized he was in that picture. Isn't it crazy how the Lord crosses your path with people, but in some situations, those people have been on the path with you the whole time? The Lord grants you awareness, not when you want it, but when you need it the most.

To this day, I firmly believe that each moment I discover different people in that picture is a moment ordained by the Lord. He orchestrated long ago the people I would need on this journey of life, preparing in advance for me the very moments they would step into. That picture of people who played in my dad's golf tournament and my epiphany moments of, "They were there too?" actually point us to something so much greater.

Jesus is always there, blazing a trail of His faithfulness and sovereignty. In the midst of tragedy, confusion, and pain, we look at the story unfolding before us and are so oblivious to the person that is always in the picture. Yet, we all have our moments when we look back, and what we were once blinded to now becomes something we are capable of seeing.

Have you ever read back through old journal entries where you angrily claimed the absence of the Lord? Then when you looked back, you saw He was there despite what you felt. He is always in the picture, and He grants you the realization of that when the time is right.

My parents spent two weeks in Mexico and then returned home. The next thing I remember was a hospital bed being moved into our home. I was confused as to why Dad was still sick.

I thought the doctors in Mexico were going to fix him.

Why does Daddy have to have one of those fancy hospital beds in his room?

I didn't know that people could have a hospital brought to them.

My dad was at his worst at this point. I didn't know what cancer was, but I knew it had a strength to it that was stronger than my dad was. At a young age, how many things are stronger than your dad? He stood a little over six feet tall, but cancer was making him small. In more ways than one. But the one thing cancer could not make small was his faith. He would not let anything do that. Cancer was his goliath, but with a heart like David, it would not make him cower in defeat.

Every summer, my family would load up either our fifteen-passenger van or our suburban. Yes, we had a fifteen-passenger van. When you have five brothers and sisters, it only makes sense. My mom and dad would hold a TV in between the driver seat and passenger seat so we could watch a movie. For six hours, they would let the TV serve as an armrest. Apparently, that was less painful than listening to their six kids talk for six hours.

The exit sign would read Fernandina Beach, and our car would veer to the right to head toward South Fletcher Avenue. Two of the houses on that road would be filled with family friends. We would spend all day on the beach, eat dinner all together, and then typically a game of Scattergories would follow. That's where we formed our love for that game.

Dad wouldn't let his weakness steal his chance for our family to live out the same tradition we did every summer. The summer following Dad's diagnosis, he was too weak to drive, so he flew down with a friend who accompanied him on the flight. We have a picture from that summer. You can see all the beach chairs lined up in a row, and then there's Dad, not sitting in a beach chair but a camping chair. I guess he needed the extra support. You didn't have to be there to know; it is clear from the picture he was sick, really sick. He weighed maybe 100 pounds. His stamina didn't allow him to make it very long out in the summer heat. How long wasn't what mattered. He was there.

There in the place that held so many memories for our family. There in the place where all eight of us spent the most intentional time together. There in the place where the ocean was the backdrop and the stars shined their brightest, all while they pointed us to a Creator who spun them into existence. You feel small standing on sand, staring out into the vastness of the ocean, looking up at the sky. But it is there that you are reminded that although the sky and the sea have an undeniable greatness about them, it is man that God is mindful of.

> "O LORD, our Lord, how majestic is your name in all the earth! You have set your glory above the heavens. Out of the mouth of babies and infants, you have established strength because of your foes, to still the enemy and the avenger. When I look at your heavens, the work of your fingers, the moon and the stars, which you have set in place, what is man that you are mindful of him, and the son of man that you care for him?" (Psalm 8:1-4)

I believe that God knew that my family needed to stand upon the shores that served as our reminder year after year that although we are small, He sees us. He knew the days we had been walking through. He knew the days ahead that were coming. He knew the narrative that was being written. He knew because He is always in the picture. That was the last trip we got with Dad.

The Day

November 21, 2002

Only my little brother Jacob and I were at home that morning. My oldest sister's boyfriend, at the time, was there when we woke up. He was soon replaced by a group of some of my mom's friends. It wasn't out of the ordinary to wake up to someone besides my mom in those days. But it was out of the ordinary for all of my older brothers and sisters to be gone too. Ignoring the setting, as any eight-year-old would, I moved into a persistent declaration that I wanted to go to school. What kid doesn't love school in elementary school?

My mom's friends agreed and started helping me get ready. It was an ordeal for them to get my curly hair into a ponytail. Finally, my hair was brushed. My teeth were brushed. Patiently, or as patient as a child could wait, I sat on the steps in our kitchen with my monogrammed Lands' End book bag. Our kitchen now has walls painted green. I think Mom did that because she knew that room would be filled with a feeling of blue for a long time.

One of the women there that morning was one of my mom's closest friends. She lived in our neighborhood, so it was easy for her to lend a set of helping hands. She answered a phone call from mom. I have always wondered what words were exchanged on the phone that day between her and my mom. I wonder if it was a drawn-out map of how to navigate the next moments with my little brother and I. Or did my mom just leave the judgment call up to her friend? She would be the one to tell the news that my father had passed. What she said? I do not know. All I know is that I can see the image as clear as day of my eight-year-old self sitting on the stairs in our kitchen with my backpack on. I think we can all look back to moments that changed the trajectory of our lives, no matter what age, and remember right where we sat. I think it is because we know the aftermath. The place where we were sitting was a seat we had never sat in before.

I would long resent my mother for the fact she did not deliver that news to me. It wouldn't be until the Lord gave me empathy for the fact my mother had to shatter the lives of her six kids and deliver news that no mother should ever have to give. Maybe it was God cutting her some slack and Him knowing that six times was just too much to bear. God's grace covers all. His grace covered my mom that day. I believe that. It wouldn't have mattered how the news was delivered, it wouldn't change what the news was. We made the drive to the hospice my dad had been staying at. This place was normal for us. Every day someone would pick us up from school, and we would spend our evenings there. It wasn't until years later that I came to know a hospice was a place people went when they were going to die.

The unknown is never something we willingly choose. As followers of Jesus, the unknown is the desert place, filled with wandering and longing for a drink to quench our thirst. The water is all the more satisfying when we have longed for it. It soothes us in a way that the immediate could not. I have grown to see the unknown as a chance to find the One I am the most desperate to know.

The unknown to an eight-year-old looked like a "not yet." The unknown would be the place that was my protection from having to face something before my mind could process it. The unknown places, the desert places, they are always purposeful. Not yet. I would later have to come to terms with what this day meant, but at the time, I was not there. Not yet. I would have to recall it, recount it, and relive it. I would understand eventually. But right then and there, I witnessed what death looked like. I just did not know what it felt like.

The hospice was broken up into two parts. One side was a hospice with a bunch of old people. On the other side of the building was a hope house, where kids with severe disabilities could come for the day, and their parents could get a break. That side of the building had a fish tank. My little brother and I spent most of our time there. The bright colors of the fish drowned out the darkness of the scene we were living. It is not a coincidence to me that the name of the place that I was most drawn to in this facility and the place I spent the seventh year of my life and part of my eighth was called "The Hope House." It pointed me forward to where I would hide in the days to come—the house of hope that Jesus builds.

In Psalm 46:1, the psalmist tells us, "God is our refuge and strength, a very present help in trouble." A refuge is a place we go to for help. He is a hope house. Even then, I believe the Lord was giving me an inclination. He could see the years ahead where I would look back and come to realize that even in the place of a hospice, He was making Himself known. The unknown was where I would find the One I was desperate to know.

I remember the drive to the hospice that day was silent. That seemed to be the starting place of the silence, and it would long stick around. It was raining. Why does it always rain on the bad days? The silence that we rode with in the car followed us in. Nothing is more haunting than silence that speaks. This was that kind of silence. I can still see where the people were sitting in the room. There were so many people in those days that there wasn't room to breath. It felt like nobody could anyway. Holding their breath, nobody knew what move to make or what words to speak. I wanted my mom. My dad's room was the second door on the left. From behind the door, my mom came out with my dad's sister. A doctor followed behind them, saying, "We are going to get him ready for them to see him." We would be presented with the chance to go in one at a time and see what was once my dad. One at a time, my siblings would go in. I would be the only one to refuse the chance.

I can't explain to you what in me made me say no, but I did. It is my biggest regret, yet at the same time, one of the best decisions I have made. Conversations with my mom following that day would make me confess that I did not want to see my dad like that. The truth is, I never wanted to see my dad sick, but I did not have control over that. To see him dead, I had felt like I had control over that, and I would take it.

My most vivid memory from the day is when my brother, Jonathan, went into the room to see my dad. He let out a scream—a bloody murder scream. I can still hear it. It finds its way through the trees to my ears whenever it decides it wants to. The scream was long and drawn out. The silence that we were sitting in made it intensified. Nobody said it, but I knew it; this is what death sounded like. The sound terrified me, bringing to life in me a fear unlike anything I had known before. That was the day fear became an antagonist. If someone asked me to describe the day my dad died, I would describe it not with words but with a sound—a scream.

Long after that day, screams would come from the mouths of my siblings. Screams accompanied by shaking a fist in the air at this God that my dad said would heal him. Screams of doubt. Screams of "why?" Screams of frustration because this was not going to be undone. Scripture speaks of shouts of joy, but that was not what these were. Shouts of joy felt as if they would never exist again.

The scream haunted me. In November of 2017, I was out for a walk in my neighborhood. There is something special about those streets. I take those walks as a chance to get alone with Jesus. I fight to leave my phone behind and only walk to the beat of the silence. Silence has been hard for me ever since the day my dad died. I don't like what it sets up. I don't like the potential of what it could bring. I avoid it when I can. When days are long and I can't seem to reach a sense of ease, I know silence is what my heart needs the most, and I have to step into it.

I go through seasons where I want so badly to remember more about that day. I beg the Lord to fill in where the gaps of memories are. I get desperate enough that I take matters into my own hands. I replay the day over and over in my head, hoping that reliving it would bring back the missing pieces. I was doing this on my walk that day. To do that, though, it welcomed the sound of the scream. I had invited it to walk with me. At times, it would show up without any prompting, but this time, I prompted it. I hate that I remember it as clearly as I do. I heard it just as I have before, but this time it came with more than just volume. It came with understanding. I made sense of the scream. I understood why it seems to find me whenever it wants to. I understood why, after all these years, it is my brothers' scream that torments me more than any other memory I have. It is because I am okay with it.

Hearing his scream keeps me from having to hear my own. If I allow myself to keep listening to his, I do not have to listen to my own. The one I know that is inside of me that has yet to come out. After facing the kind of loss I did, there is an undeniable assurance that stirring in my soul is my own sound. I have never dared to ask my brother what that scream did to him, but I want to believe that it made him be able to breathe a little bit more. It is as if I am holding my breath still, and as if my lungs are tightly contracted, fighting against my own sheer will power not to let them find liberation. Meanwhile, I am suffocating myself.

It is not the scream itself that needs to come out of me. It is the honesty. God does not need my dainty and proper false prayers. He needs the honest ones, even if it means coming a little unleashed. Naomi, from Scripture, shows us how to do this.

One thing I think so many people miss from the story of Ruth is the great loss her mother-in-law Naomi faced. She lost both her sons and her husband. Naomi wasn't hesitant to admit that she was angry with God and blamed Him. She stated three times in Ruth 1:20-21 that she accused God of her heartache. So often we are scared to be honest with the fact we are mad at God. But why? Do we think that the One who conquered the grave cannot handle someone being mad? Do we forget that even if we don't admit we are mad to anyone, He still knows? Tell Him, because when you do, He is the one who is going to come and rescue you from the anger and the pain. No one else. Just Him.

Do we fear coming unleashed like Naomi? Naomi was real with God and addressed God with her true feelings. God did not turn away when her honesty surfaced. He will not turn away at mine. He will not turn away at yours. He wants my heart, even if it is a little explosive like Naomi's. He wants my scream.

In a way, I think this book is my scream. It is as honest as I have ever been. It's a testimony to how the honesty of your struggles on your faith journey can be expressed in various ways depending on how it is best fit for you. It does not matter how it comes, it just matters that it comes.

The first day I went to counseling, I was twenty-three. My counselor asked me to tell her about this day—*the day*. She did not waste any time. She asked me endless questions. I would turn each answer back into my own question.

"Do you think it is weird that I can only remember parts of that day?"

"How can an eight-year-old remember something so vividly when it happened so long ago?"

"But why does that happen to me? Why do I remember one part more than another?"

As gradually and as compassionately as she could, my counselor gave a name to this reoccurring day that plays in my head—emotional PTSD. Emotional PTSD can be caused by traumatic experiences, like the sudden, unexpected death of a loved one.

The diagnosis of stage 4 pancreatic cancer and my dad's move to hospice gave a spoiler alert that made the loss expected to everyone else, but to me it was unexpected.

At age twenty-three, I had finally made sense of what this memory of my dad's death was. A part of me was thankful to finally wrap language around what I could never explain. But another part of me was aggravated that a diagnosis once again seemed to be the dominant factor in my life. Diabetes, cancer, and now emotional PTSD. I still do not think my heart knows what to do with it. Putting a label on this pain was tangible proof that death has effects that are continually being uncovered. A page is finally able to be turned, only to read another one that reveals more repercussions. We must drill into ourselves that we find appeasement in the fact that the page always turns. What comes on the next page might not be ideal, or what we want, but we let the sound of a turning page play in the background and softly remind ourselves, this too shall pass. The page will turn.

Though there is a vacancy in my memories, I know for sure what I did the night my dad died. At my elementary school, every month, a different grade got to perform at the PTA meeting, also known as the Parent Teacher Association. The songs were always cheesy, but our music teacher would take these performances as serious as Broadway. It was the second graders turn to do their PTA show. My father had just died that morning, but I would be at that PTA meeting.

We went. My classmates and I stood on the risers that elevated us just enough for the parents to see us. At the back of the room on the wall was one of the clocks with the big digital numbers. Underneath it stood my family and close friends. Lining the back wall, they all stood there, standing far from me yet with me. The image is still engraved in my mind today and would go on to represent what my family's portrait would look like. At times, far from one another, but still together. Seventeen years later, that image has not faded. The choice to go and sing would later become so significant when I would come to know Jesus and to know deeply the pain of losing my dad. Even then, the Lord was depositing truth into my eight-year-old heart that the Holy Spirit would bring back to mind as I got older, and the pain grew deeper: *choose to sing.*

It wasn't until I started to look back at the narrative of my life that I saw that common denominator of singing. We must choose to sing. We must be as David and sing when the unanswered questions still linger. We must choose to sing when it does not make sense. We must sing even when we stare death in the face. When my heart grows faint, and there is no song stirring in me, I look back to the day that wounded me the most and remember that I sang then. I can sing now.

> "How long, O LORD? Will you forget me forever? How long will you hide your face from me? How long must I take counsel in my soul and have sorrow in my heart all the day? How long shall my enemy be exalted over me? Consider and answer me, O LORD my God; light up my eyes, lest I sleep the sleep of death, lest my enemy say, 'I have prevailed over him,' lest my foes will rejoice because I am shaken. But I have trusted in your steadfast love; my heart shall rejoice in your salvation. I will sing to the LORD, for he has dealt bountifully with me" (Psalm 13:1-6).

That is all I know of November 21, 2002. What looked like the end of the story was only the beginning of a new chapter—one filled with much heartache and hurt, but healing would come eventually. Life would never look the same, but life would go on. The story would still continue to be written. Although with some twists and turns nobody would want.

Letters

Paralyzed.

The credits rolled, and as the people around me started to slowly gather their things and leave the movie theater, the room got smaller and smaller. There was only me, or so it felt. This wasn't a new feeling. There I sat, eighteen years old, once again suffocated because I had been reminded of all that I didn't have. And all that everyone else did have. With my heart shattered into a million pieces, my friends made their way to the exit, but the only place I was making it to was down the road of bitterness.

I felt paralyzed. But looking back at it now, it wasn't just that moment where I felt unable to take a step. I had been that way for the last ten years.

"Adria, are you coming?" my friend asked multiple times before I finally heard her. I did not speak, but I thought,

They wouldn't understand.

Nobody gets it.

I am the only one who has to deal with this.

The movie was Safe Haven. I didn't have the typical hopeless romantic moment that high school girls tend to have when they watch a Nicholas Sparks movie. It was more than that. In this movie, there is a family: a dad, a mom, a daughter, and a son. There is one specific part of the movie that took a knife straight into the most fragile place of my heart. A place I thought had been mended back together over the years.

As the movie goes along, the audience finds out that the mom passed away due to cancer when the kids were still very young. She leaves a set of letters behind for her son and daughter. A letter for her daughter on her wedding day. A letter for her son on his graduation day. A letter for the defining moments of their lives that she would miss, but she wanted to somehow speak into.

In the closing scene of the movie, the building where the letters are kept catches on fire. The letters were saved, and the fire didn't destroy them. The letters weren't destroyed that day. What was destroyed was my sense of, "I've worked through this."

The labels of the letters flashed across the screen: read on your wedding day, read on your graduation day, read on your 16th birthday, etc.... As they did, an all too familiar feeling resurfaced— *What would he say to me?*

I finally found movement and stood up from my theater chair. I wasn't alone anymore because, at this point, the workers were trying to sweep up all the stray popcorn and reset the room for the next movie. Anger is a raging fire that consumes the arsonist. That day I was the arsonist, and I was going up in flames.

I only had one thought: Why did my dad not write me letters? Why couldn't I have had something to read for the defining moments of my life? Why couldn't he have found a way to speak into my life despite not being here? Why didn't he live in the reality that he was possibly going to die and take some measures to leave things behind for his kids? Now that I am twenty-five and have lived the past seventeen years of my life without a father, there have been so many moments where I would have done almost anything to have my dad's own words spoken over my life. There has always been a never-ending desire of wanting to know what he would say to me today.

My father was a man of incredible faith. He was so confident that God was going to heal him after he was diagnosed with cancer. That is beautiful in many ways, but he also would not come to terms with the possibilities of how the outcome might play out in reality. Because of that, he didn't take care of a lot of things. There was no proper goodbye. There was no, "You will be okay." There was no letter writing. There were none of his words left behind. Before we go any further, I want to make sure one thing is made clear. Never for a second did I have to guess that my father loved me. I knew he did. This was just how the story unfolded in his final days.

Our first Christmas together without Dad was nothing more than a round of a silent game. In the days following Dad's death, nobody really ever knew whether to talk about him or not. Nobody knew whether we should highlight the fact that he wasn't there or let the absence that was undeniable speak for itself. Most of the time, the pendulum swung in the direction of, "Let's just not say anything." My mom did the best she could those days. Especially that first Christmas.

We have lots of traditions in our family, but one of them is that on Christmas Eve night, Mom gives everyone Christmas pajamas. We all sit around the fire, and the siblings exchange gifts. With five brothers and sisters, it is not reasonable to buy gifts for everyone. Every Thanksgiving, we write all of our names down on a strip of paper, cut them out, put them in a baseball cap, and take turns drawing names to see who you would buy for that year.

That year, the Christmas pajamas had been distributed. The crumpled up wrapping paper covered the living room floor as each of us had opened our one present. We each sat fiddling with our gifts as my mom and my uncle, my dad's oldest brother, came out from my mom's room. She stood with six envelopes in her hand. She explained to us that she wanted us to have something special this Christmas, even though Daddy wasn't here.

As she distributed the envelopes, I remember being so confused as to how something in an envelope could be really special. Inside that envelope was a letter. Each of us got one. Each said something different. But you knew from the time you read the very first word who it was from. Dad had written these.

That letter was pulled out of my bedside table many nights and days after we got it that Christmas Eve. Many times I would not even make it through the whole thing, and no matter how many times I had read it, the strings that it pulled on my heart would activate tears that would come and wouldn't stop. Some days I would pull it out and just read the last line over and over: *Never forget that I love you with a love that cannot even be described in words, and I always will.*

When I was ten years old, I found out my dad did not write those letters. I was devastated. To this day, I do not think there has been a moment when I was as angry with my parents as I was then. How could my mom do such a thing? How dare she try to create something that was not hers to create? How could my dad not love me enough to finish what he started? How could he not leave me anything when he had every chance in the world to? I felt lied to. I felt abandoned. I felt like the two people that I was supposed to look up to had both let me down.

I have come to see that what I really felt was that a blank page would always be the backdrop of my life. In the years that followed, I would be desperate for someone to tell me how to navigate growing up without a dad. Those words I thought my father had written felt like a road map. Then I learned the map was a fraud. I was left with nothing.

I would grow in age, and my tendency to always speak would intensify. I think that is what happens when you ache for something to be said. You want to prevent anyone else from ever having to feel that way. That would benefit me at times but also create an unrealistic expectation for myself. I do not have all the answers, and I never will, but the pain of what wasn't said spurs me toward striving to speak, no matter if there is nothing to say. I have come to learn that people don't need your answers as much as they need the journey of finding the answers for themselves. There is something about the pursuit of truth that ultimately leads us to finding what we need.

My mom further explained that my dad had started writing those letters but never finished them. It's like he picked up the pen to write but put it down and let the story end there. For so long, that's how I viewed Jesus. I viewed Him as someone who started writing my story, but the moment that cancer and a graveside entered the pages, He put the pen down. That was the end for me and for my story. All that had ever been good stopped the moment my dad died, and there would never be anything else to write about. Oh, how I was so wrong.

Jesus is the complete opposite of that. He never puts the pen down. He is always writing more. The story never goes unfinished. In fact, He is a God that is always in the business of finishing things. He made that known to us with His last words He muttered on the cross before He bowed His head and gave up His spirit. "It is finished," He said (John 19:30). Those three words are what we put our hope in today, knowing that He is not a God who starts things and doesn't finish them. He is not a God who leaves the narrative hanging when the hard chapter is being written. He is a God who is always writing. He was still holding the pen then; He is still holding the pen now.

My story and your story do not end with the tragedy and painful circumstances we walk through. The even better news is that with Jesus, the best is always yet to come. Oh, dear one, do not hang your head, He is still writing your story, and the "immeasurably more" is always on its way (Ephesians 3:20 NIV). C.S Lewis put it this way,

> "All their life in this world and all their adventures in Narnia had only been the cover and the title page: now at last they were beginning Chapter One of the Great Story which no one on earth has read: which goes on forever: in which every chapter is better than the one before."[1]

There is always more to be written.

As a child, a pen and paper were my safe place. Writing was just a thing I did. It wasn't until I was a junior in high school that I even began to share any of my words. The more I wrote, the more alive I felt. I could never wrap language around what writing was for me. People sing songs. People play sports. People make things. The effect it has on them is exhilarating. Writing made me feel more than alive. It made me heal.

The more words that have come, the more they have brought awareness as to why writing has done that for me. Writing is the way I protect my heart from the bitterness of what was never written for me. However, at the same time, writing was a constant reminder of the action my dad did not take. A game of tug of war it seemed to be. To do it brought an exhale of relief, yet at the same time, it brought a billboard statement hanging in the rearview mirror: He did not do this.

I firmly believe that your greatest pain is often the launching pad for your greatest ministry. The great pain of unwritten words activated my own written words. Writing is painful, but by doing it, I press against an old wound that will always be there. I press against it every time my fingers press these keys. It's painful, but pressing it also brings release.

Putting yourself in the position that something can rub up against that old wound of yours seems illogical, but the Kingdom of heaven is upside down. To press is to feel the release. To feel it is to heal it. To run toward it is to conquer it. The pressure of our sins bearing down on the perfection of Jesus brought release from the power of sin.

It is how the Kingdom of heaven works. It is the invitation we are given. Feel the pressure, feel the release. Trust me, I feel the pressure here and now, but every time I place a period at the end of a sentence, the release slowly but surely is felt as well. I keep writing even though I feel the pain of what was not written for me.

It Wasn't What
I Thought

The knowledge that my dad did not write the letters forced me to wrestle with the concept of forgiveness at a young age. Forgiveness is a hard thing. There is no denying that. How we come to terms with certain things and how we move in the direction of forgiveness lies solely on the extent to which we believe God is sovereign. Sovereign, in its simplest explanation, means that God is in control. There is absolutely nothing that unfolds outside of God's influence.

"For everything comes from him and exists by his power and is intended for his glory. All glory to him forever! Amen" (Romans 11:36 NLT). Everything comes from Him and exists by His power. In other words, nothing slips past His radar without Him knowing about it. God knew my dad would not write a letter for me. As I got older, I had to come to terms with the fact that I had to forgive my dad for not writing that letter. Or any letter for that matter. However, what I came to see was that my biggest problem was not my unforgiveness with my earthly father, but my belief that God had not given me what I thought I needed.

You see, we put so much blame on people. Unforgiveness is typically birthed from a place of feeling like we have been wronged. When we break down the sense of wrongdoings humans have done to us, we believe more than just that they wronged us. We believe that God wronged us. We falter in our belief that He is sovereign because if we feel we have been wronged, then really, we believe that God isn't good.

A.W Tozer says, "What comes into our minds when we think about God is the most important thing about us."[2] For far too long, I would dare to say that the first thing that came to my mind when I thought of God was, "He messed up." At the base of all my thoughts toward my earthly father, my frustrations, resentments, and so forth was the foundation that I thought God had made a mistake when it came to my story. I think if we pushed past the facades and all the cliché Christian answers of, "Everything happens for a reason," and, "God is going to use this," we would all stand side by side, at some point, biting our tongues. We say what we think we should say and hinder ourselves from saying what we actually want to say. Deep down, at some point or another, most of us have all wanted to let out the yell, "God, I don't want this."

Why do we put expectations on ourselves to reach the end of a process faster than we are required to? Why do we make everything about the finish line and not the starting line? Why do we fear that God will be disappointed with us if we tell Him how we actually feel? Why do we trick ourselves into believing that we must be okay? I'll tell you why I think we do. At some mile marker on the road we are all traveling on, we adopted this mentality that in order to suffer well for the sake of Christ, we must not acknowledge the suffering at all.

There is nothing more I love to tell people than simply this: You are allowed to hurt. If that were not true, Jesus would not have wept with Mary and Martha at the tomb of their dead brother Lazarus. He wept with them (John 11:35). He knew they were in pain. He didn't tell them to stop, but He joined in with them. I found myself falling into the trap of "things we are supposed to do as Christians." What it inevitably did was prevent me from moving forward because I was not acknowledging how I really felt. Oh, how much time I would have saved myself if I could have taken my hand off of my mouth and let out an honest prayer to the Lord years ago. Maybe I would have realized a little sooner that my issue wasn't with my earthly father but with God.

My issue was with God and my lack of belief that He is sovereign. I did not have a hard time believing that God existed. However, I just could not wrap my head around how a God that is supposed to be so loving could let something so bad happen to me. It is the go-to argument of unbelievers: How could a loving God allow suffering? There are components of that question that no man will ever be able to explain fully.

God did not have to prove Himself to me for my faith in Him to start to rekindle. What had to happen was I had to see where I was and then let Him take me where I needed to get to. I had to vocalize to Him that my belief in His sovereignty was at its weakest point, and I needed Him to help my unbelief. We can become blinded by our circumstances, and I was blinded. I had been asking for so long to see the answer to the question, "How could you have let this happen?" But what I needed to be asking was, "Jesus, would you show me yourself?"

When we see Jesus, everything changes. When we come to know His characteristics and attributes, it enables us to start to make peace with our stories. All I had to do was simply ask Jesus to give me sight once more to see Him for who He is: sovereign, perfect in all of His ways. He is constant, never-changing. He is good, and if He is never-changing, then He is *always* good. I knew this, but my heart rejected it because to believe it was to believe that there could be good in my father's death. That could not be. Surely that was not possible.

Years later, my mom apologized to me for giving us those letters. She told me that she believed her children needed a word from our earthly father and that our hearts would find rest in his words. She said that her vision was so skewed back then to think that any word other than the words from God, the perfect Father,

was what we needed. Ye...
from a father for their hearts...
perfect Father could have filled i...
   I went on to discern that for so...
something I actually did not need. I longed...
to speak something over me when no one perso...
to say what we need. As followers of Jesus, we must...
our minds on one specific thing we think we need be...
inhibits us from seeing everything else that is happening. It clo...
our vision to the possibility that Jesus might have done or spoken
long ago what you are looking for, just in a different way. He gives
us what we need, though it is often in an unexpected form.

What we have is what we need. Scripture tells us in Matthew
6:32, "For the Gentiles seek after all these things, and your heavenly
Father knows that you need them all." God knows what we need. If
you break that down even further, you find that if God knows what
you need, then, if you don't have it, you don't need it.

As humans, our hearts long for a lot of things, but deep down,
I think we all are on a quest to discover we are loved. I think that
is why I gravitated toward that last statement most in the letter I
thought my dad had written: "Never forget that I love you with a
love that cannot even be described in words, and I always will." We
want to know there is a banner of love hanging over our lives, and
there is. It is a cross. It is the greatest "I love you" that is and ever
will be offered. When we stop seeing the cross, we start to look at
what we don't have.

I lost sight of the cross the day I watched Safe Haven. The
anger that birthed in my heart that day was a wildfire. It didn't just
take days to put out, it took years. My heart shifted though—a shift
that was brought about by the simple thought of how many other
girls were out there that were not only without a father too, but
were without that same letter I dreamed of. When our hearts make
that shift from anger, resentment, pity, and sorrow to acceptance,
our hearts soften. When our hearts soften, they become open and
willing to see purpose.

ss started to
dset deviated
moments of my
chance to speak
what we struggle
of meaning in our
s always purpose in
ards acceptance, and
forward into allowing
might be looking for.
ded to walk through the
ad something from my dad
nto the countless girls who

her children did, in fact, need a word to find rest. But only the words of a the emptiness that was there. many years, I longed for for one specific person holds the power stop locking cause it

IT IS WRITTEN

are a

My bein , sovereign was restored. I was seeing Him once n been a myopia contrived in my life, and it was my pain. It p ced me from seeing any rightness. There had been a defect in my competence in identifying how the equation worked when it came to my relationship with Jesus. I am never the one who does the forgiving in the relationship. Our awareness of His sovereignty is our awareness that He does not wrong us. He is the only one who needs to forgive because He is the only one who has been truly wronged. We are the culprits of the crime, and the good news is He always forgives.

I can't write you that letter that would be from your dad, but I do have a voice. I do have a, "I've been there." I do have a, "Me too." I do have a, "I've felt the same way." I do have the power of the Holy Spirit to be the translator to string sentences together to form not the letter you have dreamt of but still a letter. I do have the title of an overcomer of those hard moments. I do have the comfort that Jesus has shown me, and everything He has taught me on this journey. I have all this, and I will not be selfish with it. I will share it. I believe that God, in His complete sovereignty, allows us to walk through suffering so we can turn around and walk through it with someone else.

This, this is part of the good that I thought was impossible. This, this is the chance for me to walk with you and remind you over and over that your story does not end where you are right now. This, this is God using the pain. Let me walk with you. It would be my honor.

Maybe you are like me. Maybe your dad knew that his days were numbered and yet still chose to leave behind nothing. Maybe you aren't like me. Maybe your dad had no idea that his days were coming to an end sooner than ever imagined. Maybe your dad isn't physically gone, but emotionally he is unavailable. Maybe your dad is there, but he chooses everything else before choosing you. Pick any of them, and I can assure you a daughter who has a father that is absent in any way is longing to hear something, anything.

I have been unsure for so long what exactly these pages were supposed to look like. For five years, I thought this book would be a collection of letters that I would write to you, and at first, they were. There was a "read on Father's Day" and "read on your birthday." It mimicked what I saw in the movie Safe Haven. They were written with the intent for girls to one day read them, but after processing many things, I came to know that those letters weren't written for you. They were written for me.

In the summer of 2017, I was sitting in the parking lot of a Mediterranean restaurant listening to a podcast by a pastor in Miami, titled "Lost Letters."[3] The message was from 2 Corinthians 3:2-3, which says, "You yourselves are our letter of recommendation, written on our hearts, to be known and read by all. And you show that you are a letter from Christ delivered by us, written not with ink but with the Spirit of the living God, not on tablets of stone but on tablets of human hearts."

You are the letter.

I have been bearing the weight of trying to write these letters to you, not knowing that my life itself was the letter. These last seventeen years since losing my dad is the letter. The letter has been written and is being written. To retell of those days, to share this life of mine with you, to lay out my journey of growing up without a father—that is the letter. It is not in the form of "dear you," but it is a letter. I wanted to give you something to read on the defining moments of your life and speak truth into those days. I missed it for so long that His mercy, love, and grace that pushed me forward through the muck and the mire of those days is a letter in itself. To simply let you have a glance of what those days looked like is to let you read a letter.

It is not a letter from your father. That was the gap I was trying to fill that was not my place. However, I know that God did not need me to write you a letter. He has written a letter through the days of my life. What He has written is far better than what I could ever write. I will recall and recount what this life has looked like, what the Lord has taught me through this. In some ways, yes, this is just my life, but because of what is being recounted, I pray that you can read these words when you face similar days and be encouraged. This is my story. This is my letter to you.

The promise that our life is a letter fuels my faith. It is a reminder to me that when I thought the story was over, with my father's death, something was being written. It reminds me that although the blank page has always felt like the backdrop of my life, the pen of Heaven was at work. To look back is not only so I can write, and you can hear my story; to look back is for me to read the story God has always been writing. This is the chance for me to read the letter my heart has been longing for all along. A letter from my Father, coming in the form of my own story. This is for you, but at the end of it, this is for me. There is no greater resource we can create than one we know we needed ourselves.

Don't you see it? The letter from your Father has been written. It's the story of your life. Maybe you should look back too and let Him read to you. You will see His faithfulness woven through every day, and you will be reminded that even in the darkest of places, He is the light. He can still write in the dark of the night. Someone once told me that if you ever doubt God's faithfulness, re-read your own story. I'm writing so I can re-read it. There is no such thing as the letter that was never written, not with Jesus—It Is Written.

Father, speak now. They need to hear from You, not me. You have written and are writing this letter of mine. Help me to tell it.

Braveheart

September 19, 2017

Every word on these pages has required me and will require me to go back to painful moments of my own life. Some of them have been easier to revisit than others. However, this story, this event, this step, it was the one I have fought and fought. Not just through the process of writing this book but through life in general. The moments that wounded us the most are the moments that we have to go back to because sometimes going back is what propels us forward.

We see this to be true in Scripture. We see it in Peter, the bold disciple. He was willing to declare Jesus as the Messiah when nobody else would. His declaration of Jesus would then turn to the denial of his association with Jesus. The setting of the denial, a fire.

> "Then they seized him and led him away, bringing him into the high priest's house, and Peter was following at a distance. And when they had kindled a fire in the middle of the courtyard and sat down together, Peter sat down among them. Then a servant girl, seeing him as he sat in the light and looking closely at him, said, 'This man also was with him.' But he denied it, saying, 'Woman, I do not know him'" (Luke 22:54-57).

Jesus would go on to be crucified and resurrected. Peter would see Him again. In a different place but with a familiar backdrop. John 21:9 says, "When they got out on land, they saw a charcoal fire in place, with fish laid out on it, and bread."

It is the first interaction Peter has had with Jesus since he denied Him, not only once but three times. Jesus knew how much those denials wounded Peter. I do not think it is a coincidence that He took him back to the very setting where it first happened. It's as if Jesus wanted Peter to go back there, to the actual physical place where it happened, and deal with it. I don't think Jesus was trying to rub it in Peter's face. He was not trying to press and mash on a wound to make it hurt worse. Instead, what He was really trying to do was set Peter free from the enslavement that place had on him.

I was Peter on this particular day. I sat around my fire of coals with Jesus and went back to the place that wounded me the deepest. I can count on one hand the number of times I have been to my dad's gravesite. Really, this day was the first time I legitimately went there since my dad died.

It had been almost fifteen years, and that place had a hold on me. It wasn't that I was afraid of it but more that I was afraid of how it would make me feel. I had been praying for about a year for God to make it clear to me when the time was right. I knew there would be a day that I had to revisit that place, but I did not want to do it just because I felt like I should. I only wanted to do it because I knew God was inviting me there. This day—September 19, 2017—was that day.

Any other time I have been to the site, someone has driven me there. I found it interesting that it had been so long, yet I needed no directions. I still knew how to get there, but don't we all? We all know where that moment happened for us. The moment that made us question God's goodness and existence the most. We all know where it is yet are hesitant to visit it. I get it. Why would we? Why would any of us want to go back to that place? Because going back is a way of us being able to see not just the depth of the wound but the extent of the healing that has taken place. Going back allows you to see where you once were and where you are now. Going back is what takes the blinders off and enables you to see that Jesus has been working.

To not go back is to stay blind. To not go back is to cheat yourself of the awareness that you have never walked alone. To not go back is to miss a chance to have breakfast with Jesus. The One who does not want to make you feel the burn from the fire but wants to let you be nourished by it. Jesus offered Peter breakfast that day. He did not have him sit there, sweating from the heat. He is far too good for that. Jesus nourished him. Only Jesus could take the moments of revisiting our deepest pain and make them something that nourishes us instead of making them something that stings us.

I could see again this day. I drove there in silence. I knew that I needed that time to be still and to communicate with Jesus. Driving there was remembering this road I had been on for the last fifteen years, but remembering led me to something more. There was an undeniable feeling and assurance that Jesus had been on that road with me the whole way through.

I remembered the day of my dad's funeral as we drove to that gravesite. An eight-year-old little girl, peeking out the back window of our car, behind us a line of cars, following us. There was no end in sight. They kept coming and coming. That sight has been a tangible reminder for me that so many people have been with my family on this journey, and so many people individually have been with me.

As I got out of the car at the gravesite, I kept walking around trying to find my dad's name. When I could not find it, I started to get frustrated. A man who worked there came up and asked me if I needed some help. I told him I was looking for someone, but that it had been a long time since I had been there. He said to me, "Oh, that's okay, we can help you get there." The man walked me in the right direction, and as we got closer, he said, "There it is." Then he let me go on my way by myself. I believe that there are places that we must go on our own. Others can sometimes have a keen awareness of the steps we need to take, and they can hint at a destination. However, ultimately, Jesus is the only one who can point us in the direction of where we need to go. His prompting and stirring are what make us step. No man can get you there. Jesus invites us there.

He invited Peter in the direction of where he needed to go by making the fire. He stirred my spirit and made it clear it was time for me to go to the gravesite. You do not have to be afraid or worried about being unsure of how to get to that place. We do not have to know. We only have to be willing. From our willingness, He will then take the role of a navigator and direct us not only to where we need to revisit, but He will lead us onward.

I stood there, facing the reality all over again. I stood there, with a strong sense of "I miss him" resurfacing. I stood there, with my shadow overlapping the words, "Gregory Elliot King." My shadow was big. I was tall. This was Jesus' way of telling me that the little girl that first visited that place did not stay there. He has been working in me. He has been shaping and molding my heart. He was showing me that life did not end for me that day. It has gone on. It has been hard and painful, but death was not the end of the narrative. Things did not stop that day. The story was not over. My story was not over. I had grown. Through the tragedy, I had grown.

Through tears, I said, "You are okay." It was not how I felt that made me want to say that. My heart was sad, tears streamed down my face. Our feelings have their own things they want us to say. It is our faith that produces the unexpected responses in moments of heartache. My belief in the promise of heaven spoke in that moment. I knew that my father was an incredible man of faith. I knew that his gravestone was a reminder of his departure from earth but also his arrival to heaven. He was okay. He was with Jesus.

Our belief in heaven is built off our belief in the resurrection. As breath filled back into the lungs of the crucified Jesus, the invitation to partake in a heaven song was offered. We now had access. We now had a new way to think. Death would not be the end for us anymore. Without the resurrection, we would be hopeless. We know that the tomb is empty. The resurrection did happen, and because of that, eternity and the heavenly realm are offered and promised to all who believe. Heaven is not just a place; it is a promise. John tells us in Revelation 21:4-5,

> "'He will wipe away every tear from their eyes, and death shall be no more, neither shall there be mourning, nor crying, nor pain anymore, for the former things have passed away.' And he who was seated on the throne said, 'Behold, I am making all things new.' Also he said, 'Write this down, for these words are trustworthy and true.'"

There will be a day when this pain will be no more. There will be a day when all things are made new. When we put our trust in that and believe in that, we realize that we, too, will be okay. I walked away from the gravesite that day, saying, "I'll see you soon." This, this is not it. Heaven awaits us, and in heaven, all things will be okay.

You, my dear one, you might not feel okay in this moment, but you will. You will never stop missing what you have lost, but your perspective will change. The pendulum will ever be swinging from one side to the other. Until I arrive at the gates of heaven, I will sway between the tension of, "I am okay," and, "I am not okay." There is freedom to swing back and forth. Some days feel easier than others. Yet, in an instant, you feel like you're back where you started. That is just what grief does.

We stand firm on the hope that Jesus will make all things new. In the here and now, we wonder if that moment will ever come for us. A moment where we can permanently say, " I am okay." We do not have to wonder forever. When we arrive on the shores of eternity and look into the eyes of our Maker, our souls will rest. We will be okay.

I drove home from the gravesite, listening to a song they played at my dad's funeral: I Can Only Imagine by MercyMe.[4] The lyrics talk about the moment we finally get to the feet of Jesus. What will we do? What will we say? I can't help but imagine my earthly father at the feet of Jesus. Completely cancer-free, more alive than he has ever been. That thought makes me grateful for a God who has created a place where cancer is no more.

My dad is okay. Knowing that only reassures me that even in death, Jesus is working. Until the day when I find myself at the feet of Jesus, I will beg of Him to daily remind me of the promise of heaven. Until that day, I will only imagine what it will be like. I'll keep letting my imagination run wild, and I'll now actually take steps forward. I was courageous enough to do what I had long been terrified to do: go back. However, I know that by going back to that place, I am all the more prepared to take you to those places with me. You will read many stories that are "then and there," but there is a "here and now." It would be a failure to not mention those too. Here and now, courage became mine to claim.

On my dad's gravestone, it reads, "Forever our Braveheart." Braveheart was my father's favorite movie. It is a romance tale of a man who became a widower and then gave his life fighting for the freedom of Scotland. The main character's name is William Wallace. His name travels far and wide. People speak of his name out of awe. William Wallace was brave. His heart was broken from losing his wife, but he did not let grief steal his courage. Instead, he went on to fight for something greater. Through his grief, he fought.

There is a William Wallace in all of us. There is a person who can fight through the fog. There is the one who can choose faith instead of abandoning it. There is brave in all of us. My father fought cancer with his faith never faltering. He was his own kind of brave, but my dad is not the only Braveheart. I am a Braveheart. You can be a Braveheart. I don't know what that looks like for you, but I hope you go for it.

In the opening scenes of the movie, young William Wallace stands by the grave of his father. A little girl comes up and hands him a thistle. A thistle is a purple Scottish flower. In the midst of death, what she had to offer was a flower. Not words, not answers, but a bit of beauty amidst the tragedy. I like to think it was her silent way of saying, "Remember, there is still good."

For all my days to come, I want my loss to be used as a thistle. I hope my presence around someone is a reminder that there is still color. I pray that people will know there is good because God is always good. I've tasted and seen His faithfulness. I've felt His healing and comfort. May what He has done in me be so evident that it is a thistle to someone else. I hope by now this is starting to feel like what my heart longs for it to feel like—like we have been on a journey together. The journey of navigating through life without an earthly father figure present. I hope this feels like me meeting you where you are and handing you a thistle.

Six Sides

The old saying goes, "There are two sides to every story." That seems to be true for most stories. In the case of my family, there are six sides to this story. There are six of us—six kids, that is. Three girls and three boys. In order from oldest to youngest, it goes Anna, Allison, Joseph, Jonathan, Adria, and Jacob. Try to say that as fast as you can. It is always a fun game to play with new friends.

During the final years of my dad's life, he was named one of the top sales reps for his company. With that came a trip for our entire family to Banff, Canada. My dad was too sick to travel at this point, so my mom asked her sister to take his spot. All eight of us loaded a plane at Hartsfield Jackson airport in Atlanta and flew to Canada.

As we rounded the corner where Banff Springs Hotel was tucked away in what felt like its own separate world, my eyes grew wide in wonder. I had never seen anything like this place. My mom very seriously said, "Do not touch anything when we go inside." This was not a place where people were accustomed to having kids as guests, especially six of them, two being under the age of eight. But this place was every kid's dream. Unlimited snacks and soda; we never got soda at home. Two extra dollars per person added up. During our stay at Banff, the activities that were offered ranged from horseback riding, hiking, dog sledding, and white water rafting. Jacob and I were seven and five at the time, so what we were able to do was limited. My older siblings, along with my aunt, would go and do things older kids got to do, and Jacob and I would stay with Mom.

That's where it all began. The division between us. The older kids would do their own thing, and Jacob and I would stick back with Mom. Mom liked to call us Frick and Frack because after my dad died, we would go with her wherever she went. For years, that was what it was. Every man for themselves and then there was Jacob and me. We always stuck together. We had each other. We had no idea how true that would be in the days to come.

Grief is a monster. There is no way to sugar coat it. Some say no grief journey is the same. That would prove true with my siblings. Their grief came in different forms—having a baby, alcohol, and painkillers. I do not share these stories with the intent for you to feel sorry for me. And I do not share all of the details because, in the end, these are not my stories to tell. I share them because some of you will resonate with one of my siblings more than you resonate with me. Some of you will leave this chapter feeling a little saner because you will know that it is okay for your grief process to look different than those around you. Some of you will even have a better understanding of your loved ones.

I share because my siblings' paths, at times, all seemed like the end of the road. Their journeys stretched my faith and at times left me hopeless, but in the end, hope was always found. The story of what was once lost but is now found is always something to be shared. What seemed like the end was never the end. Some of you need to be reminded of that as you walk this process of grief on your own but also alongside others. You need to be reminded that Jesus comes through.

My oldest sister Anna used to lifeguard at the neighborhood pool across the street from where we lived. I loved to go to work with her and walk over to the clubhouse where I could order chicken fingers. Anna was the one I gravitated toward the most after my father's death. I would send her emails full of incorrect punctuation and all the spelling errors asking her to take me places or if I could sleep in her room for the hundredth time. Don't let the ability to write fool you. I have never been able to spell, and I still can't.

In fifth grade, I was at work with Anna one day when she told me she was going to have a baby. The news would not settle the same for me as it would my other siblings. I love kids. I was ecstatic at the news. However, I now know that I, per usual in these times, did not understand what was unfolding. My brother Jonathan had just returned from a summer camp and had been updated on what was going on, and it wrecked him. Anna moved out of the house and lived with her boyfriend. If there wasn't already a massive gap in our home, now it only grew. As it grew, so did the tension and the distance between my siblings and me.

On February 9, 2006, Anna gave birth to a beautiful baby girl. Anna is a writer herself, and she would later describe this time. Her words would come a decade later, in an email when I asked her to write for my blog. The email she sent to my inbox became a message the Lord sent to my heart:

> "On June 6, 2005, I was eighteen, soon to turn nineteen the next month. The day was hot and humid, characteristic of a Georgia summer. The air in the South becomes stifling and thick when we move closer towards the sun. My summer Spanish class began at 9:30am, and I was halfway into completing my Bachelor's degree. Clenching the pregnancy test in my hand, pink lines crisscrossed slowly, indicating I was pregnant. Since November 21, 2002, I had been a fill-in parent after my father died. I chose to forfeit moving away to college since my mom needed help driving the kids, but

I suspect she also needed my emotional support. I rose to fill the need, since I had always been a natural leader and thrived on being able to provide stability and security. As a young girl, I remember making schemes preparing what to do if anything happened to my parents. I strategized I'd put all of my siblings into the red Radio Flyer wagon and would pull them myself the three or four miles to a trusted friend's house. When some of my siblings were really little, they would get up at night and sleep in my room when they were afraid after Dad died. I disciplined. I went to school events. I set schedules. I coordinated pick up and did laundry and simply carried out whatever needed to be done. Even with the turmoil of watching my father shrivel from cancer, I kept good grades, stayed out of trouble, and got a scholarship to a local college, where I continued to excel. I listened to every terror and fear, squabble and delight my beloved brothers and sisters brought to me with a tenderness reserved only for them. And then, what I later described in a poem as the "jugular hold on ambition that [hid] the loneliness," disintegrated when I learned I was going to have a child."[5]

Anna's words gave me that perspective, a perspective that I wish I had learned long before. It is tempting for us to disregard the pain of those who are causing us pain. The feeling of Anna abandoning us shortly after my father died never allowed me to see Anna's pain. We cannot let our pain do that to us. We cannot let it make us unaware of the pain of those closest to us.

Anna went on to graduate college, all while having a newborn and working a part-time job. The sweet redheaded baby that would grow up within the walls of our childhood home would be a soothing joy to our family. We would catch our breath. The tide would settle for a significant amount of time until the next wave of grief would hit again.

My sister Allison, with her blonde hair and blue eyes, would catch the eye of any boy. I asked my mom time after time if she was adopted, and my friends would ask me the same thing. She graduated high school and loaded up to drive the three hours to Valdosta State University. Allison was three hours away, and that made it hard for me or really for anyone to know how she was doing. The credit card bills soon enough let us in on what was hiding—a drinking problem.

Allison graduated from college and had intentions to stay in Valdosta, but my mom said otherwise. She brought her home, and everything that had happened in Valdosta would now be known to all of us. I was in my first years of high school, and at this point, I was hiding too. What was happening in my household was so different than what anyone else my age was dealing with that I felt like an outcast. I shared very little with people those days. How many sixteen-year-olds can understand the effects of grief? Our "perfect" private Christian school did not leave much room for people to struggle. The struggles were viewed with judgment and not grace. I would not give people the power to judge my family. There were too many emotions already being felt, judgment could not be handled.

That same Christian school would be where Allison stood on a platform and let what was in hiding come out. I have learned that the enemy lets what is done in secret become strongholds. Allison had come to share about modern-day slavery at our chapel but ended up sharing about her own slavery. Up until that point, I still knew very little of her journey. I knew she was home. I knew she had problems sleeping, but I did not know the depth to which it went until then.

Allison suffered from severe insomnia, but it was so much

more than that. She would tell the room full of high schoolers that she remembers so vividly the night before my dad died being so tired yet so afraid to go to sleep because she knew what she would wake up to. This only intensified as she went off to college. Going without sleep will make you crazy, desperate. Her solution was to pick up the bottle. She would drink until she passed out.

Eventually, she would find true freedom, true rest, but it would be in the person of Jesus not in the comfort of another drink. In that moment, as she shared on stage, I no longer feared judgment. I was proud. That was the moment it clicked for me. I realized then, by the testimony of my own sister, that our mistakes and struggles are not something that God turns away from in disgust. People might do that, people that are not walking in grace, but God does not do that. He delights to take our struggles and make them our strengths.

This was a revelation not just of what God was able to do but of who He was. He was compassionate, forgiving, creative, able. He took the mess and made a message. Allison shared with courage that day. For the first time, I felt like I knew my sister, and to know her was to be able to have empathy for her. This time the calm would be short-lived. My family would breathe again, but only to have the breath completely knocked out of us.

Bridges of Hope

I was the most aware of my siblings' struggles during the next wave, or what felt more like a hurricane. This one hit hard. I had graduated high school and was old enough to fully comprehend the circumstances. Addiction. Even the pronunciation of that word makes it hard for me to swallow. You see drug addicts on TV or hear of these things called rehab facilities that are advertised like they are some resort. You grow to have a new view of addiction when someone you love is in the middle of it. Addiction is engulfed in darkness. Where there is darkness, there is a greater fight to believe. Jonathan came first. We would later find out that both Jonathan and Joseph were facing the same battle. On January 13, 2014, I wrote in my journal,

"I'm tired, Jesus. Tired of nights spent outside my room, listening to Jonathan and Mom argue. Jesus do something, please. I hate drugs. I hate them. Help me, Jesus. Give me hope. Deliver him. Jesus, help me to believe you are able because right now I don't know how to believe. When I am faithless, you are still faithful. Come into the broken pieces and somehow mend them, Jesus. He doesn't even feel like my brother anymore, and I want my brother back. I don't know what to pray. I don't know what to ask. I just need you, Jesus. Fill in the emptiness. Make your presence known. Come for me, Lord. Come for them."

Addiction feels like a round of the silence game with the Lord. The more control it felt like the darkness took, the more relapses that happened, the fainter my heart grew. Prayers got shorter.

Three-word prayers seemed to be all my lips could mutter after months of nights sitting outside my room with my little brother Jacob. We would sit at the top of the stairs next to the balcony, and I would say the same thing over and over, "I trust you." It was all I could get out. It was all I had in me. It wasn't much, but it was enough. It was a battle cry. My words and my heart might not have been lining up, but I knew that it was all I had left. The darkness of addiction was trying to pry my fingers off my hope in Jesus. Almost as if I was climbing a mountain, struggling to hold on to take the next step, and the darkness would come up behind me and a little at a time loosen my grip. My continuous repetition of that prayer and of the declaration that I would trust Jesus kept me holding on.

I did not dare tell my friends what was happening inside my house. I stopped inviting people over, fearful that they might have something stolen from them while visiting. Addicts steal. They lie. They manipulate. They are willing to do whatever it takes to ensure that they can purchase whatever they think they need to get through the day. My resentment was not for the watch that was taken and pawned, or the camera, or even the cash taken out of my purse. My real frustration was that these painkillers my brothers were using were creating havoc in our already broken home.

This wave of grief had all of us drowning. The first rehab for Jonathan didn't work. The second one didn't work. Hope would be found momentarily, only to be lost again. Even when he used again, I could not let myself settle for believing that God could not do a miracle. Instead, I read every verse I could about Him being the light. Psalm 107:14 is circled in my Bible with both of my brothers' names written in the column. "He brought them out of darkness and the shadow of death, and burst their bonds apart."

Jonathan got arrested in April, right around the time my oldest sister was set to get married. He would not be in attendance. You would expect that the joy of a wedding would be capable of taking all of our minds off of what was happening behind the scenes. The enemy wouldn't allow that to happen. My sister got married at the courthouse. The Clayton County jail was the building next to the courthouse. We couldn't run from it. Jonathan had just left this place to head to his fourth rehab.

The word hope would silently be the flag that would always wave on the shore when we were still in the boat being tossed at sea. The hospice my dad died at was the Hope House. The rehab facility that my brother would attend and become sober at was called Bridges of Hope. The Lord has this way of weaving messages into our circumstances, messages that He knows we will not even see until maybe decades later. He writes them anyway. That is a signification of His character; generous and kind. He knows the very word our hearts long to hear sung, and He sings it even when we are incapable of hearing. He knows at some point we will tune back in. He delights to keep playing. He does not grow weary in the repetition but instead rejoices when we get one step closer to seeing the message that has been there all along.

As I'm writing this, Jonathan is now almost six years clean. He has married the woman of his dreams and is pursuing Jesus. The darkness would not steal him from the light forever. It had its time with him, but Jesus, the light of the world, would go into that darkness and pull him out. Only He was capable of doing it, and only He gets the glory and the praise for the success of that rescue mission. Our family's celebration over this victory was momentary as we would be faced with a rematch of the same beast.

Joseph's addiction unfolded much differently than Jonathan's. Joseph was a master at hiding. No one would have ever been able to know the state he was in unless he confessed it. We often look with disgust at the ones who are far out there and blatantly in sin, but at times, it is those in hiding who have a greater uphill battle. You cannot fight back against what you don't identify as an enemy. You will not defeat something you are too afraid even to speak out loud. What happens in the dark can never be brought into the light without a confession. Their fight was against the same monster, opioids, but the darkness came in a different shade with the secrecy Joseph walked in. He, too, would attend Bridges of Hope. As his sister, all I could do was pray and wait.

I waited, with weary eyes and hands that sometimes felt as if they couldn't carry what this world handed me. I waited, with vision blurred by tears, uncertain of how this pain of mine would play a part. I waited, with confusion that was spiraling into doubt. I waited, straining to see over the horizon, wondering when the sun would start to rise. I waited, standing in a field of darkness, peering up into the night sky, longing for the stars to come out so I could dance in the moonlight. I waited in a silence that somehow managed to speak hopelessness. I waited, crippled by my fears and growing hesitancy to even try to take the next step. I waited, cold, shivering, treading through the snow, asking, "Will this winter we are in ever end?"

I waited, but I kept reminding myself; He's coming. The King is coming. When He comes, our eyes fill with wonder, and we get to open our hands and lay down the load. When He comes, weeping doesn't blur our vision but instead gives way to new sight, and we see that He weaves pain into the fabric of our story with a purpose. When He comes, doubt is overcome by the discovery of an empty tomb. When He comes, the sun does rise, but not just the sun, the Son of God. When He comes, the stars come out fiercely, all hundreds of millions of them, shining in a dazzling brilliance and we dance in that open field of ours. When He comes, He puts breath back into our lungs that we will use to sing a new song. When He comes, the chains of fear fall, and we not only feel the confidence to step, but to run. When He comes, the snow melts beneath our feet, and winter becomes spring. We wait, but He's coming. The King is coming. Hold on a little longer. Don't lose heart, dear one. He is coming. He always comes.

Joseph would be a resident at Bridges of Hope for seven months, and he would get clean. He would come home to live in a home with other recovering addicts. Months later, my mom would be thousands of miles away visiting Jonathan, who had moved to Idaho to work on a ranch. I was working a part-time job for a lighting company and received a phone call at work. One of our neighbors had called and revealed some information that made all the signs point to the fact that Joseph had relapsed.

If you asked me to pinpoint a moment when my hope felt the most diminished, this would be it. After everything we had gone through to get to this point, we landed back where we started. Some might even consider this as grounds to completely give up on believing who Jesus said He was. I cannot deny the fact that I considered it. The question I typically get when it comes to suffering is, "Why keep believing?" My answer is always the same, "If not Jesus, then what?" If I had let go of my faith in that moment, there would have been nothing left in my world that was secure. There would have been nothing left to motivate me to push forward. There would have been nothing left for me to put my hope in that addiction would not be the end of the story for my brother.

Another round of rehab was not an option financially, but the love of a younger brother for his older brother would go to extreme measures to find an environment that would allow his brother to become sober. Joseph would also move out to Challis, Idaho. In a single bedroom apartment, with two twin beds, Joseph and Jonathan would live. They would get up every single day together, stand next to each other physically, emotionally, and spiritually, and they would go to war to fight against the same thing, and they would win.

Joseph has now graduated with a degree in Nuclear Engineering. He is the patriarch of our family since the passing of my dad, and nothing has been more beautiful than to see him step fully into that role. He was unable to truly do that until he dealt with the brokenness that was within him. When you swim through the waters of unresolved pain and grief, you reach the other side and find there is the version of you that Jesus has always intended for you to be. Pain wants to steal your potential. Fighting through it gives you even more. The enemy tastes a little bit of defeat every time we are willing to swim to the other side. Both of my older brothers now stand as men of God, pursuing Him and trusting Him.

I once served on a panel for high school girls that centered on the topic of broken homes. A girl, who must have been no older than fifteen, asked me about what my grieving process for my dad looked like. My answer instantly went into all the different things my siblings did. She did this, and he did that. Mid-sentence I realized that I was talking about their processes because I did not have one of my own. The realization came as I verbally processed years of my life and some of their choices. It led me to stand face to face with the reality that I was no different than my siblings. They did anything and everything to avoid the pain of having to grieve my dad, and I was doing the same thing. Mine just did not play out the way theirs did.

Avoidance was the theme of each of our stories, but I never took the time to stop and look in the mirror, and that prohibited me from seeing that I was one and the same with my brothers and sisters. I was no better than them. I had no place to judge them. I, too, was avoiding the grief. The next morning, I called my oldest brother and told him about what happened and apologized for the way I judged him and looked down on him at times. He graciously accepted my apology and posed the question, "So what will your grieving process look like?"

23 going on 8

At age twenty-three, I was becoming a child again. Jesus told us to become like a child when we come to Him (Matt. 18:2-4), but the child in me was so broken. The wounded child in me was stuck in a hospice room as an eight-year-old. To let myself become the child was to allow myself to feel that level of brokenness that I had been masking as I got older. To feel broken, to know you are broken, to live in that place for a time—we so often think it is a bad thing. Brokenness is not a *bad* thing; it will actually *benefit* you. Brokenness will not belittle you. In the end, it will *better* you. The realization of your brokenness leads you to the realization that you are not the one who must hold all things together. Only Jesus can do that, and only Jesus was meant to do that. "And he is before all things, and in him all things hold together" (Colossians 1:17)

You, my dear one, are broken. You are completely powerless to hold yourself together. By coming to a place where you see this, you can come to a place where you can surrender it as well. As you loosen the grip on trying to "hold it all together," you release yourself from the presumed expectations and pressures. You come to find rest in the truth that the only thing you need to hold onto is Jesus. He takes you, every little piece, no matter how broken or fragmented your heart may be, and with hands that bear the scars, He holds all of you together.

I robbed myself of so much over the years by thinking I had to hold it all together. I now know I was falsely holding myself together, but at the time, I believed that I was, in fact, doing so. By striving to hold myself together, I was unable to hold anything Jesus had been trying to give me over the years. In the church, we often hear the term "open hands." It's coming around this concept that we need to pry our fingers from the earthly so that we can receive what Jesus is trying to give. It is twofold—our hands are open, saying, "We want to receive from you," but we are also saying, "Take whatever needs to go."

In my youth group, they would ask, "What are you holding on to?" Like any typical teenager, I would roll my eyes and whisper under my breath, "Nothing." However, now I see that for far too long I exhausted myself with taking the broken pieces of my heart, shoving them in my hands, and clenching my fists so nobody could see them. By doing so, I missed so many chances to receive. It wasn't that God wasn't giving. It was that I was too afraid to let go.

Maybe even now you have been begging for God to give you something. I challenge you to evaluate yourself and make sure your hands are, in fact, open. Open hands don't just mean materialistic things. It means the releasing of comfort, of stability, of dreams, of facades, of unforgiveness, of resentment, of bitterness, etc....I think we probably all need to loosen the grip a little bit today. I think we all probably have something hidden underneath our clinched fist that we have been hiding not only from the world but from ourselves.

I wonder if the boy with the five loaves and two fish stood there in all his innocence as a child, wondering how Jesus was going to use what he had. I think he probably did because I know I do. But the same thing Jesus said to the disciples that day, "Gather the pieces that are left over. Let nothing be wasted," (John 6:12 NIV) is the same thing I imagine He says to us. That's what He does. He uses the pieces. He uses the broken places of our hearts. He doesn't let any of it go to waste. However, He can't use them if we don't hand them over to Him. We cannot hand them over to Him if we hide them. Unclenched fists, open hands, receiving what He has for us.

The main thing I was hindering myself from receiving was my identity. He calls me daughter. He has been calling and always will be calling me that. I was too busy being what I thought I had to be and missing who I actually was called to be. The moment I unchained myself from the responsibility to hold it all together was the moment that I started to walk in freedom for so many reasons. But mostly because the releasing led me to be able to receive the name He has been persistently whispering over me all these years: child.

You hear people tell stories of their childhood. You listen as they talk of times when the air around them seemed to have a sweeter aroma. It is as if their days of youth held a little extra something that livened up their insides. They recount scenario after scenario of when they were totally and completely childlike. When the opinions of those around them were inconsequential and their inquisitiveness kept them dreaming.

It is there inside all of us, that child. The one we like to tell stories about. The one that wanted to be a doctor on Monday but by Wednesday was ambitious enough to claim an astronaut as the goal. Cardboard boxes were our transportation to anywhere we wanted to go. Hairbrushes were our microphones on the largest stages. We now speak of that part of us in the past tense. Memories we like to reminiscence about. However, this part of us, this version of us. It was never intended to be spoken of only in the past tense form. It was always intended to stay.

I feel as if I never was the child at all. Maybe you feel like your childhood was robbed completely from you. You had to grow up too fast. You had to step into areas no kid your age should have had to. At age eight, my father died, and when he died, it felt like my childhood did too. There is nothing but a thick fog up until the age of eight. In many ways, it feels as if that is where life ended but also began. Maybe you are similar. I know this is not the truth. However, it is all I know. So now, as I take a deep look into my reflection, there is no clear picture of who I am. There is only distortion, and I have chosen to live in it. Yet, the Lord has been dropping handfuls of rocks into the pond, interrupting the falseness of my beliefs, and crafting a new reflection. I am embarking on a journey to discover who I am. What I've always thought about myself is being dismantled by the kindness of the Holy Spirit, who loves us too much to let us stay where we are. He will not settle for a false self. He will not settle for the misconception of identity. He will keep at it for those of us who are His children who are serving as an amnesiac understudy.

We so often forget. We often see wrong. We often settle for what we have always known. What we have always known does not constitute as grounds for the right way of living. There is a better way. I now know that what I long for most in the world is not to be seen. It is not to be known. It is not to be applauded. It is to have a childhood. It is what so many of us are looking for. With Jesus, childhood is not a page in the book that we turn. Childhood is the whole story. To get what I have always wanted, I need only to step into what He has been offering all along.

I came broken before Him, handed Him a million pieces of me. He gladly took them all, and then handed me the first of so many things. He handed me the very thing that I thought was gone forever. He handed me the very thing that my heart ached for the most. He handed me the title: child of God. A child has a Father, so by Him handing me that title, He was also handing me the assurance that I still have a Father. I do not go without. You do not go without.

Have you ever had that moment when you leave the house, get halfway down the main road, and realized you forgot something? You have to turn around, go home, and the process of starting off on the journey kicks off all over again. My mom would do this all the time growing up, especially when we were leaving for the beach. We would be loaded up, with more than half of our house with us, and finally start to pull out of the driveway, only for her to remember that she forgot something. I am convinced that few things make me more frustrated in life than when you have to start over on something when you thought you were finally well on your way down the road. That is how grief has felt for me.

When you lose a parent at such a young age, nobody tells you that the reality is that you will basically face death twice. Once when it happens, and again when you fully grasp it. I encountered it again when I was twenty-three. I thought I was well down the road, but the Lord revealed to me that was not true at all. He needed me to start. I was only concerned about finishing. My goal-oriented self has a real struggle with perceiving something that does not come with an end goal or a finish line. I knew where I was at on the journey—the very beginning—but I was straining my eyes to look off into the distance to see where I was trying to get to. Grief does not have a finish line.

I didn't see the point in working through something that was going to be there for the rest of my life. I didn't see the point in trying to deal with something that was going to resurface at times. I didn't see the point in trying to walk through the valley of the shadow of death if it was just a valley that I would have to reenter. The grieving process seemed like money I would waste on counseling sessions and tears that weren't necessary to cry. Being so young when I lost my dad, a part of me feels like I never knew him. If that is the case, what am I even grieving? My mind was twisted, turned, and jumbled into sheer doubt. I doubted that this mattered anymore. This perception of grief is extremely toxic. I knew it was toxic, but it didn't change the fact that this was my thinking.

In the summer of 2018, after working a summer of camp, I drove down to the beach with a friend and shared with her where my heart had been. I gave a disclaimer that before I said anything that I was fully aware of how dumb it all sounded and how she was going to say, "Are you serious?" when I told her about struggling with the thought: What am I even grieving? Like expected, she reiterated that my thinking was not coming from truth. She also told me that it would make sense why I would feel this way. She reminded me that afternoon that what I was grieving was today.

In this journey, every single day you are grieving the here and now because the here and now is not what it typically would have been. We have permission to not just grieve what was but also what could have been. When I looked around at the aftermath of death amongst my family, a part of me felt like I did not have the right to grieve. If I could not even remember my dad, how could I be sad? I was waiting for someone to hand me a permission slip, not realizing that the permission slip came in the form of a God who offers us the freedom to feel. I was grieving the fact that I would never know what it would be like to have an earthly father present. I was grieving what never was.

As the years keep going by, I will have to keep grieving the "today" because the days will never look like they could have or how I expected them to be. A part of me felt even more defeated because now, every day, I have something to grieve. But another part of me felt like where I was made much more sense. I was grieving the loss of what I thought life was supposed to be for me.

I told my counselor that it baffled me to think that five years from now, I could be in the same place with processing my father's death as I was right now. She asked me where I wanted to be five years from now. I told her that I didn't want to be dealing with it. She tenderly told me that it sounded like I was refusing to accept this was part of my story. She was right. I did not want to accept this. I felt like this loss of mine was tattooed on my forehead. It was the ace up my sleeve that I had to pull out every time someone got close to me because they needed to know that every now and then, a side of me might come out that might entail a little bit of sorrow.

You will always be incapable of moving forward if you will not accept what has been given to you. Acceptance does not mean that you are receiving the platter with a twinkle in your eye that says, "I wanted this." Acceptance does not mean that the loss you are facing is not real or affecting you deeply. Acceptance doesn't even mean that you don't wish it could have gone down another way. I think about Jesus in the Garden of Gethsemane moments before He would walk the way of suffering. "And going a little farther he fell on his face and prayed, saying, 'My Father, if it be possible, let this cup be taken from me; nevertheless, not as I will, but as you will'" (Matthew 26:39). His honest cries were paired together with His obedience.

His agony and desire for the way things were about to go down to be different did not dismiss the fact that He was living out the purest form of acceptance we will ever know. His acceptance was on display with His heart cry, "Nevertheless not as I will, but as you will." I don't want this to be the story. I don't want to go the rest of my life knowing that my dad will not be a part of it. I don't want to face any more hard days. I don't want to keep working through this. But more than I don't want any of that, what I really don't want is my will. I want His.

Grief is not about being able to check off a box on your to-do list. Grief is about my walk with the Lord. Grief is about my perception of Jesus holding firm and true even when the wind blows me toward a destination that I did not want to sail to. To throw the towel in, to say that it is not worth it, is to settle for stagnant faith. To forfeit and keep wondering what is the point of all of it is to rob myself of the chance to have intimate encounters with the Lord in the resurfacing of the same pain. Grief is about grieving what was lost, but it is also about realizing that in a never-ending journey, in a never-ending process, there are never-ending possibilities to experience the wonder of who Jesus is. He is a never-changing God, but He is also infinite. He never falters in who He says He is, yet He manifests Himself in different ways in the different seasons that we are in. There is far more to Him than I know. There is far more to Him than you know.

Grief is a full-on boxing match with round after round. We can't forget, though, in Him we win. What we win might not be the thrill of crossing the finish line, but it will be a deeper awareness and understanding of the person of Jesus.

Other than Scripture, the books that have ignited my faith more than anything are The Chronicles of Narnia series. Something about the simplicity that C.S. Lewis used to explain who Jesus is through the character of Aslan helped me make more sense of who Jesus is. The children who get to interact with Aslan, the Great Lion, are the Pevensies. The land of Narnia is magical, a place the children always longed to be.

We are all like the Pevensies, dreaming of the land of Narnia, where the sun is warm and the winter ends. We must not forget that it wasn't Narnia the children's hearts longed for the most. It wasn't the land itself that had the magic to melt away the snow. It was Aslan. You long for a person more than you long for a destination. That is why to leave a place of sorrow and run to the perceived safety of avoidance will never satisfy you like running to the person of Jesus. That is why to give up on the grief process won't give you the satisfaction that you are looking for. Tackling your grief, fighting this fight—that's what will lead you to what your heart is really looking for: a person.

Grief is a doorway that will lead you straight to Him every single time. It is an assured, guaranteed arrival at the place we all desperately want to be—close to Him. Who knows, maybe, just maybe, if grief was something that we could "accomplish" it would stop us from going to Him as often as we do when we are in it. To me, the most beautiful part about my grief is that it has the potential to normalize someone else's grief, to make them feel like the things they are feeling, the thoughts they are thinking, are not really all that crazy. Grief is hard and painful, but it is worth it. I know that I still have a lot to figure out about this whole grieving thing. At least I know what my starting line looks like: the confession that I am a broken child in need of my heavenly Father to mend my heart.

Halle

During my junior year of high school, the community where I lived was slim, and loneliness was a real feeling that I grew to know all too well. Thankfully, I had an amazing friend who I had met at summer camp in fifth grade that became a life-long friend. At the end of the day, I knew I had at least one person in my corner. We both were desperate for some Jesus-loving people. She had started attending some youth stuff at a church in Atlanta and invited me to go to their weekend winter retreat, a weekend I will never forget. Over the next year, that church would become my home church.

Junior year quickly became senior year, and I found myself in a place where I not only wanted to attend church, but I wanted to serve. I wanted to give back and make a way for more people to experience what I had gotten a taste of. Being only a seventeen-year-old, I was not sure what I had to offer, but I knew that I had to get my foot in the door somewhere and somehow. The church I attend calls their volunteers "door-holders." They are coming around the idea that you are opening the door for someone else to enter into the church. Week after week, someone from the staff would mention signing up to be a door holder, but my insecurity kept me away from the application process for a long time.

Finally, I bit the bullet and started my door holder application. There was one thing that I knew I didn't have to question: I loved kids. Coming from a big family and doing babysitting jobs for various families had birthed in me a love for kids that was significant. I filled out the application to volunteer in the kids' ministry and from there challenged myself to take the mentality: wherever you want me, Lord.

My computer made that sound. You know the sound when the email has been sent? Off it went, my application. I had no idea what that was going to lead me to. I heard back from my church faster than I expected. After a background check, a series of questions, an interview on the phone (they take their volunteers seriously people), I was set to serve for my first time. When I got the email to confirm serving for my first Sunday, they had assigned me to kindergarten girls. I arrived, and the familiar face of a girl I knew brought ease to my nerves. We would be leading together. I thought,

This won't be so bad.

The little girls are so cute.

I am leading with someone I know.

Those were all the things I thought to myself. If there was a scale for comfort that day, mine was at the top of the scale. This was right where I was supposed to be. Or so I thought...

The next week I was assigned to first-grade girls. I hesitantly clicked yes to the invite in my email, and the nerves that had been settled with the familiarity of a friend serving with me had been reborn. I saw my friend that morning and asked if there was any way I could be moved back. She explained that she had no idea why they had moved me or who to talk to about getting me moved back. She had no idea, but God knew.

It was my very first day with first-grade girls, and it was Halle's first day too. Of course, I did not know her name was Halle then, but I would learn that quickly. Have you ever had that moment where you look across the room at someone, and you can't seem to figure out if you know them or not? You know, when you keep awkwardly staring and keep running through the possibilities of how you could know them? That was me that morning and the Sundays to follow.

Halle came to church every other Sunday. However, I was only serving every other Sunday. God did that. Aligned our schedules in a way only He could. I couldn't put my finger on it. I was drawn to Halle. Of course, she was the cutest first-grader you had ever seen. She listened during the lessons. She responded during group time. She was always the last to leave, which meant I got to spend the most time with her. Yet still, I didn't know what it was about her that kept making me gravitate toward her.

One Sunday, while waiting until the parents came to pick up their kids, I was sitting with Halle, one-on-one, asking her some questions to find out more about her. I asked her what she had done over the weekend. She told me that her mom had rented a hotel room in Atlanta, and her and her brothers went and swam all weekend in the indoor pool. I followed by asking her what her parents did for work. The answer Halle would nonchalantly give teleported me.

"Well, my mom doesn't work, and my dad used to have a job, but he died last year."

It was like I was going down the hill of the roller-coaster. It was like I had been transported back in time ten years. For a split second, I could only see myself standing in the middle of an empty room. But it wasn't the eighteen-year-old me; it was the eight-year-old me. Halle was me. She was the exact same age I was when my dad died.

When I came to, I let out a soft smile and responded to Halle by saying, "I lost my dad when I was your age too." As a child would, she looked up from her coloring sheet for a split second and just said, "I hate when that happens. Don't you?" I whispered under my breath, "More than you know."

I was drawn to Halle because I am a firm believer that one of the greatest things you can have in common with someone is suffering. Or to have a deep pain that comes from the same place. Halle and I passed the genre of "in common" and were instead walking down the same road, hand in hand. There are so many people in this world longing for someone to say, "I get it," to them. That Sunday morning was the morning that I got to offer my understanding of something that was unfamiliar to most.

Halle wouldn't fully comprehend it in that moment, but I did. I understood Halle, and one day, maybe even as she reads these words, her eyes will be opened even wider to the significance of that moment.

I was put in that first-grade girls room, where I didn't want to be because God knew it was exactly where I needed to be. God was revealing to me a deeper purpose. It was more than just volunteering at church every other Sunday. He was showing me the purpose in my pain. He was allowing me to be the very thing I had longed to have. I was getting to be someone else who knew what it meant to lose your dad.

The question we are most likely to be pulled toward when walking through loss is *why?* It is as if the moment we walk away from the gravesite, we take the first step on our quest to discover meaning in our suffering. We set out on an expedition hoping the island that will come into sight is an explanation. Do not think you are in that boat alone if you are there or have been there. I sailed those same seas, looking, begging, asking Jesus to bring justification to my pain.

As I write this, I am thousands of feet in the air, flying back from spending a long holiday weekend in Paris, wiping tears away from my face, hoping the woman next to me does not notice. I look back on moments that were silhouetted with darkness, where the only thing my voice could find to utter to Jesus was, "Why?" Nights where the emptiness and absence of an earthly father was too much for a teenage girl to bear. Nights where words were few, but the ache in my heart was a heavy load that no one could bear. It was in those moments that I felt the tears serve more than just as an indication of pain. The tears served as a washing of my eyes to pave way to new sight. I would grow to see that Jesus was not and will never be afraid of the honest cries of my soul.

When we dare to get honest about how we feel, it does not drive Jesus away. It does not birth a disappointment in Him that causes Him to write us off. No, my friends, what honesty does is let Him deal with what He is already fully aware is there. It lets us hear His answer to the question that you resisted to ask.

The story of Jesus with Lazarus, Martha, and Mary shows us His heart for us broken people. However, the way Martha boldly speaks to Jesus is something that more of us can relate with than we care to admit. As Jesus approached Martha and Mary, after the death of their brother Lazarus, Martha let out a phrase that encompasses what many have thought but never spoken out loud. Minutes later, her sister Mary would speak the same declaration out into the open. We have already learned from the story of Martha and Mary that Jesus weeps with us, but another significant take away from the story lies in the words of these sisters.

"Martha said to Jesus, 'Lord, If you had been here, my brother would not have died" (John 11:21). Then it's Mary's turn a couple verses later. "Now when Mary came to where Jesus was and saw him, she fell at his feet, saying to him, 'Lord, if you had been here, my brother would not have died'" (John 11:32).

If only we would have the courage to fall at His feet and cry out what so many of us have thought and felt. "Lord, if only you had been here." Our pain is blinding, but sometimes our grief paves way to sight. Martha and Mary could not see what Jesus was doing and would do. We are incapable of seeing what He is doing at times. As Martha and Mary embodied honesty, the outcome was that Jesus wept with them.

The Messiah sat with them at the tomb of their brother, weeping with them. For Jesus to weep with them, I imagine as if He was saying that He knew it hurt. Maybe as we long for some sense of comfort in our trials, being honest with Him is what will break down the barrier and lead us to feeling Jesus is not so far away, but instead realize He is there with us. Even at the grave, sitting with us, weeping with us. He wants us to be honest. Honesty opens the door for Him to meet you right where you are. And for Him to meet you is for you to not necessarily receive an answer to your question but to receive something better—a person. That is what

I have to offer you today, not answers, but a person. He will do and give what no answer could ever do. He will weep with you. He will comfort you.

Our longing for reasoning—answering the why—sends us into a spiral of doubts, believing that God won't ever use the broken places. However, He does. We might not ever fully land on the island of an explanation. We might never get the full answer we want, but God paints things in the sky as we sail the seas. He puts us in certain situations so that we get the chance to say, "This is why."

Halle was a "This is why," moment for me. Halle was the climax of clarity in my suffering. She was the epitome of God being kind and giving me more than I deserved. I have to come to terms with the fact that Jesus does not owe us an explanation, but in His kindness, He graciously gives us moments where we can put the pieces together, even if it is only a little.

I could hardly contain myself that day as church came to an end, and Halle's mom came to pick her up. I wanted to talk to her mom more than anything, but the timing was not right.

During my days of serving, I was also in the leadership group with the student group. Once a month, the students would meet and converse about the things the Lord was doing. We were having one of our monthly gatherings, and after one of our small group leaders shared, our student pastor asked if anyone else had something they wanted to share. I nervously volunteered. Nothing made me more nervous than public speaking (this will be comical in the pages to come), but I knew this story had the fingerprints of the Lord all over it and to not share it would be a shame.

I told the story of meeting Halle and how my heart had found such an ample amount of peace in the days following that moment. I told the room that for so long, I had wondered what good could possibly come out of my father's death, and for the first time, a glimmer of perspective was shining. I knew that if anything I could tell this little girl she was not alone. I could tell her what no one ever told me.

My small group leader was in the room that night and heard the story. God being a God who connects the dots, my small group leader was in a women's Bible study with Halle's mom. While attending the Bible study one week, she asked Halle's mom if she had heard about me. Not to my surprise, she hadn't. My small group leader explained a little bit to Halle's mom about who I was and what had happened between Halle and me.

One Sunday, after the five o'clock gathering at church, Halle's mom stopped me as I was leaving the auditorium. I would later find out it was unlike her to be at the evening gathering, but she was that night. I was making my way out of the auditorium when our eyes made contact, and she waved me down. I walked towards her, and we embraced in a hug. She knew my pain, and I knew hers. It didn't require a conversation to obtain that knowledge. The word "loss" informed me of everything I needed to know.

She thanked me for being so good to her daughter, for loving on her, and for offering myself to serve the way I was. We began to talk about our backstories, and she asked me for a few more details about my story than what she already knew. I explained to her that I had just turned eight in October and that my dad died a month later in November. She asked me if I remembered what day it was. Of course, I remember. It is a day I'll never be able to forget.

"November 21," I said.

She took a slight step back, and her eyes got bigger and filled with tears. There was a pause, almost a gasp. With a shaky voice, she responded,

"That's the same day my husband died."

The day Halle lost her father. The day I lost my father. The exact same day. We both cried and were at a loss for words. In my mind, I was thinking, "This cannot be happening, there is no way." This was the work of Jesus. He is the only one who could bring together a decade in an instant. The only one who could write out details of two people's lives with such similarity.

It had been ten years. Ten years since my dad had died and along came this one little girl. Losing her dad not just at the same age as I was but on the very same day. Standing face to face with her mom, I knew again; this is why. I can show this little girl there is hope in Jesus. I get to tell her that she will be okay. I get to tell her that she is not fatherless. I get to tell her that someday she will say, "This is why." I get to tell her that maybe one day she will meet another little girl and will cry tears that aren't of pain but of understanding.

Not only was Halle my "why," she was God's way of showing me that where Halle was, was where I once was, but as a perfect Father He has carried me through all these years, bringing me to where I am now. It was God rolling the film for me to watch back on those wounding moments of "why" to see that there was another character in the scene with me. He was always there. Pain, loneliness, and darkness would not be what silhouetted the nights anymore. Jesus would be what silhouetted the nights. Halle was where I was, but Halle was not where God let me stay. She was a reminder to me that: This is not where you stayed.

More than anything, I wish I could roll the film for you. I wish I could make you believe it when I say it: He is there. Depending on what you find yourself walking through right now, I know that is a concept that is easy to read, easy to say, but so hard to believe. Let me stand in the gap for you. Let me say it a million times. Let me sing it into your darkest nights. Let me remind you of Halle.

Jesus sat at the tomb with Martha and Mary. He did not dismiss the way they felt or tell them to get over it. I come from the same place today. I'm not telling you how you feel is wrong or that it is time to move on, but I am telling you that how you feel is not an indication of the truth of Jesus. He is omnipresent, always there. I do not know what it will take for you to believe that once again. It took me encountering a little girl on a Sunday morning and hearing her say the words, "My dad died." What I do know is that if you want it, it is offered. If you want it, you can ask for Him to help your unbelief.

It is time. It is time we forfeit the wrestling match against honesty and let it win. It is time we let honesty have a seat at the table. Jesus told us, "I am the way, and the truth, and the life" (John 14:6). Honesty leads to Him. He is honesty. It is not too late for you to believe once again that He is there and that He was always there. It is not too late for Him to paint something in the sky for you. It is not too late for you to experience your own "this is why" moment. He always brings purpose to the pain.

Hear me when I say this though, meeting Halle was a gift that I did not deserve, but it took Halle for me to realize that it is not an answer we need to look for, it is just Him. When we find Him, we will see that He never lets the pain go to waste. When we see Him, we see the scars on His hands that point us back to the cross. The cross says the greatest pain a person could endure did not go without purpose. In fact, it was that great pain that gave way to the greatest blessing we could ever receive. Forgiveness from our sins, eternal life, hope, love, and something to remind us that our God is greater than death. If there is a death in your story right now, it is no match for Him. Jesus is greater. Maybe, just maybe, after we let out that prayer of, "Why?" we then need to start changing our prayer to, "God let me find you." Because it is Him we really need.

This story was on my lips for weeks and weeks. I could not get over it; I don't think I ever will. I finally decided to head to my little corner of the Internet, where my very unprofessional blog was located. It had all the grammatical errors and, most of the time, no organization, but I thought I was C.S. Lewis. I quickly wrote out the story of Halle in a simplified version and posted it on what used to be adriaking.blogspot.com. To remind my soul of His goodness, at times, I still make my way back to that post and giggle at how not well written it was. However, that in itself is a lesson for all of us. A story that has Jesus in it does not need to be told in an eloquent way. Just speak. His work is enough in itself to pull people in.

More views and more views. The post was spreading like wildfire. To this day, it is one of my most read blogs. I kept checking the stats, and for a while, thought there was a glitch in the system on Google or something. I remember telling my older brother about the views, and he did not even believe me until I pulled it up for him. People were reading this story, and they were moved by it. The blog would keep up the momentum for days.

A couple of days after posting, I was fishing with my little brother when my phone rang. The caller ID read the name of my student pastor. I was confused and thought maybe it was an accidental dial. Being the kind of guy he is, the first thing out of his mouth was him jokingly asking what I was doing. I responded, but I really wanted to say, "Why in the world are you calling me?"

He proceeded to tell me that my pastor had read my blog and wanted to tell the story to our church. He asked me if I would be up for that. I said yes. The total time for this phone conversation was maybe five minutes. I did not know what it would look like for this story to be told to our church. A text message sent a couple days later extended an invitation for me to come and sit down with my pastor, his wife, Halle's mom, and my student pastor.

I had never met my pastor before, let alone had a conversation with him. At the meeting, my youth pastor greeted us, and my pastor and his wife came into the room shortly after. They exchanged hugs with Halle's mom, which made it clear to me that this was not the first time that she had been around them. My pastor looked at me and said, "Adria, tell us a little about your story."

I think I could have thrown up in that moment. I had no idea how to tell my story. I had never really done it before. I had written it out but never spoken it verbally. I told the room about my dad, my family, my journey with the Lord, how things happened with Halle. When I finished, Halle's mom told her perspective of how the story unfolded. Then my pastor simply said, "We want to tell this story, and we want you to be the ones to do it."

By this time, I figured it might be a good time to ask some details of what this meant. I came to find out it meant all three gatherings at our church, in front of thousands of people, where Halle's mom and I would be interviewed, along with one of her close friends. This friend was a component of the story that I was unaware of up until this point. She was actually the reason Halle's mom was even attending this church. She had heard Halle's mom's story, and her heart went out to her as she too was a mom the same age as her with three kids. She asked around to a couple of people and finally landed on Halle's mom's email address. She sent her an email, and they connected. All this led us to this moment.

I walked away from that meeting that day having said yes to sharing this story on stage. To this day, I am confident that it was only by the power of the Holy Spirit that I said yes that day. Nothing in me wanted to. I HATED public speaking, and the thought of doing it in front of that many people was nauseating, but yet I still said yes. It is like the Lord knew taking the stage that day would prepare me for things to come way down the road.

Sunday came. I was as nervous as any human could possibly be. I would meet Halle's mom's friend for the first time and be brought to ease. Her presence was calming, and she reinforced that God would tell the story, not me. I only needed to do what I had done already—be available. That day—June 14, 2013. It lit a spark in me. A spark that would not be fanned until later on, but it was lit. The day came, and it went. It ended with my pastor's wife looking me in the eyes, saying, "You might hate public speaking, but you have a gift, so you need to get over it." I brushed it off and thought nothing more of it. Until years later, I found myself taking a job for the summer of 2017 at a Christian camp where my job would be to speak from a stage every single day.

Halle's mom and her three kids moved to Atlanta, and I started nannying for them and continued to do so over the next year. There were many days and many nights spent in that home with those three kiddos. Nights that typically ended with me sitting in what we like to call the "breathe" room, praying this prayer: "God you did not forsake me on this journey, and You will not do it to them. I have nothing to offer them, but if anything, through my life, let them see that they will be okay."

I got to walk through a lot of life with that family as I spent time with them. Significant days would happen, and there were so many things I wanted to say to Halle at different times, but I knew she was not old enough to receive it. They were words that had been stored up in my heart that the Lord had spoken to me. During the months spent babysitting those kids, I would remember that day I watched the movie Safe Haven, and it prompted me to start writing things down for Halle in a journal. All the things I wish someone had said to me about this journey of growing up without an earthly father.

The more I wrote, the more I started to recognize that there are a lot of us out there. A lot of girls who have dads absent from the picture. Despite our assumptions that we are the only ones, we are, in fact, the farthest thing from the only one. It did not stay what it started out as, but it did start there. It started with Halle. Halle led me to this. Halle led me to you. I never doubted that God would use my story, but Halle was the little extra push to put it down on paper. You will see stories of her all throughout these pages. She served as a trigger to memories of my own that would enable me to wrap language around moments that I am now writing about.

I must leave my time at this computer screen as I am on a plane flying back from a weekend getaway to L.A. with a friend. I started this chapter on a plane back from Paris. I ended it on a plane back from L.A. Some journeys take longer than others. You are always taking ground, though. We are about to touch back down in Atlanta. As we take ground, I pray that you do too. New ground. New steps. I shut my computer today with a prayer rising up in my heart for you: *Lord, give them a "This is why," moment.* When He gives it, let Him use it—whether on a stage, on a page, in a small group, at a dinner with a neighbor. Share it, friends. It will change you, and it will change others.

My Father

I love to travel. Call me crazy, but a friend and I started concert hopping for Justin Bieber and found ourselves going to multiple continents to see him. Yes, you read that right, continents. My college years looked different than most as I decided to stay home and commute. It gave me the opportunity to be able to travel in ways I would not have done otherwise. Those adventures that I got to take and the places that I got to visit, they came with lots of time to think. There was so much space to sit and reflect. There is something about new places. Anytime I travel somewhere I have never been, I pray the same prayer, "Lord, show me something new about You here." He did every single time.

When I was in Australia, my friend and I rented a car and drove down Greater Ocean Road. It is one of the most memorable things I have ever done. We drove the whole day and made stops at different markers to get out and take in the scenery. I spent most of my time looking out the window at the most breathtaking sites as we road in silence. The ocean danced alongside the road, and no words needed to be shared between us. We both knew this was majesty and yet started talking about a place we knew that was far more breathtaking than this.

Heaven became the conversation that day. My friend said to me, "I bet you can't wait to get to heaven to see your dad." I went to speak, but words did not come out. I thought I would respond with a resounding, "YES!" Tears started to roll down my face, and I had this visual. Yes, I can't wait to get to heaven to see my dad, but in that moment, I was seeing a new sight. I could see my dad meeting me as I entered into heaven. I could hear him telling me how proud he was of me, but then I could hear him say, "Come on, I want you to meet the real Father." My dad's eyes stayed in the same direction the whole time. He wasn't looking at me; he was set on keeping his eyes on where he knew Jesus was.

Growing up, I knew about Jesus. I came from a family that spoke of His name freely. It would not be until my dad died that I came to know the Lord in a real way, but even after encountering Jesus for the first time, I spent so many of the years following missing one important word: MY. As I stared out that window, driving down the coast of Australia, it all seemed a little surreal—the thought of heaven and the newfound thinking that in heaven what my heart awaits the most is not to be reunited with my earthly father but to meet my heavenly Father.

My heavenly Father. I had no problem identifying God as a Father. I could spit out the Lord's prayer, "Our Father..." For so long, though, I missed that there is another personal pronoun that I get to put in front of it. Yes, He is *the* Father. Yes, He is our Father who is in heaven. But, He is *my* Father. By the blood of Jesus, He made a way for me to come back in, to belong to Him. Through the confession of my sins and belief in who He is, I belong to Him. He belongs to me. This is good news.

I think a part of me always knew this. I knew that I could call Him my Father, but it felt hard. It felt like I was passing over the fact that I had lost my dad. Maybe it was saying the word "father" out loud that felt like a foreign language. Or maybe it was because I had let myself believe that part of my world had died, and I had no right to a father. I am not exactly sure what it was, but I do know that when I finally let myself call Him mine, everything changed. To let myself have that word flow from my lips again was healing—my father, my dad. Although my earthly father was no longer present, God was not asking me to go the rest of my days without being able to call someone what my heart was longing for. I still had a Father.

It was February 15, 2014, and I was spending the day babysitting Halle and her siblings. Halle was running around. She was playing with some friends who had come over and said, "I wish we had a time machine so we could go back before daddy died and him not have to." She didn't mean for me to hear her say it, and I don't think she even knew I heard her, but I did. The blunt statement she let out was that childlikeness in her that was not afraid of her feelings. We have days, days where it's simpler than we are making it—we miss them. The people we have lost. We miss them.

I had a dream about Halle's dad that night. Halle's dad was dropping her and her brothers off at the house, and I was waiting on them. He hugged the boys and told them he loved them. Then Halle ran to him, jumped into his arms, and squeezed him as tight as she could. He whispered into her ear that he loved her. Halle turned and ran into the house with a huge smile across her face. Their dad turned and looked and me and said, "Keep their eyes on Jesus." We all have to keep our eyes on Jesus because He has the comfort we are looking for. Paul lays it out for us:

> "Blessed be the God and Father of our Lord Jesus Christ, the Father of mercies and God of all comfort, who comforts us in all our affliction, so that we may be able to comfort those who are in any affliction, with the comfort with which we ourselves are comforted by God. For as we share abundantly in Christ's sufferings, so through Christ we share abundantly in comfort too" (2 Corinthians 1:3-5).

It is not, "Will God comfort us?" It is not, "Will God show up in our affliction?" It is PRAISE be to God who is the God of all comfort. It is PRAISE be to God, who comforts us in all of our affliction. You do not praise someone for something they might do. You praise someone for what they have already done.

Paul calls God "the father of mercies." To take the words more literally, Paul was stating that God is the originator of all mercies, the source from which they flow. I cried a lot of tears that week, especially after that dream. As always, the tears brought forth new sight. That Sunday, I drove home from church and could not help but think about seventeen years ago when my family stood in the midst of death. Then I looked at where we are now, and I did not just see the faithfulness of God but the comfort. I wish I could say that in the middle of the hard times I was aware of all that the Lord was doing, but I wasn't. I am more aware now. There is beauty in being real with a world that needs you to be honest with them. There is beauty in saying, "As obvious as it might have been I missed it."

I did, I missed it. I missed the fact that in the darkest days, God was still the God of all comfort. I missed the fact that in the sea of grief, God was still the originator of all mercies. I missed the fact that He was being a Father to me. We pray for Him to be those things to us, but He already is. Paul says, "Praise be to Him." He was the God of all comfort all those years ago when Paul wrote this letter to the church in Corinth. He was the God of all comfort seventeen years ago when my dad died. He was the God of all comfort in some of my darkest days. Today, He is still the God of all comfort. Right now, God is still the God of all comfort.

There is one single tree in Halle's front yard. The kids love to climb it. The youngest would always get frustrated when he couldn't make it as high as the others. There is a room in their house that lets me sit inside and still be able to see what the kids are doing. I watched Halle climbing that tree one afternoon. What is it about trees? As kids, all we ever want to do is climb trees. We want to go higher than where our parents tell us to stop. We like the thrill of the challenge. We like to climb upwards. When we climb trees, we look up the entire time, focusing on the top, because that is where we want to get. That is life: climbing, trying to make it to the top, focusing on looking up. For us, as we look up, we focus on Jesus. Today, keep climbing. Keep looking up. Keep your eyes locked on Jesus.

Those days where we do find ourselves with a longing for

things to go back to the way they were before, they make us long even more for the days where we don't have to miss those people. We must keep our eyes on heaven, knowing that every step we take here, every new height we scale in our tree climbing, is just shortening the distance. We are almost home.

Oh, little girl, I hope you know today what it took me so long to realize. Jesus delights in hearing you say the words, "My Father." He has always been willing to be your Father. You have the freedom to start addressing Him as what He has wanted to be for you all along. It is in Him you will find comfort, the very thing I know you need. I am climbing on. Will you join me? *Jesus, help us to keep our eyes on You even when we don't want to. In the middle of so much pain, help us to keep climbing, to keep looking up, reminding us that one day we will reach the top. We will reach You. The Father, our Father, and my Father.*

I Am Sorry

It has been a while since I have mustered up the courage to open up this Word document. 30,000 words have hidden amongst the college assignments and Internet searches for "Adidas tennis shoes." I hid these words not because I was ashamed of them but because they scare me. A few of my closest friends know about this little project of mine. At this point, they have stopped asking about it because I think they want to avoid the side of me that will be defensive and give them every excuse in the book as to why now is just not the time. They do not ask, and I wouldn't either. A part of me doesn't believe this will ever find it's way to you. I don't think I have what it takes. I don't think I can do this, but I want to fight to try.

It was football season. I gathered with friends to watch the Super Bowl, and by watch the Super Bowl, I mean we were really all there to see Justin Timberlake do that half time show. These friends are old and new. One was a childhood best friend. Others were friends I made in my twenties. We tried to keep track of first downs and who was winning, but the conversations led elsewhere. Cheers from the crowd and referee whistles became background noise to a more significant event. We talked of big dreams. Specifically, the song one of them was about to release to the world, a song that is vulnerable and honest. I had been having a lot of conversations with this friend about her believing the lie that people won't like what she puts out. I had given all the pep talks about why that was not true. As we all sat there sifting through the fears and the lies she was letting herself believe, internally, I was saying, "Me too."

I was thinking it. I was feeling it, but I was not verbalizing it. We give the enemy power he doesn't have when we live in fear. We intensify that power when we are terror-stricken of even the confession of fear. Silence leaves too much room for the enemy to use words as his arsenal. His words are coated with kerosene, and to listen to them is to let our faith be burned to the ground. We hear him too much when we give him silence. Silence can be destructive to your well-being. It has been to me. Worship and praise will break the silence and allow us to take back what is rightfully ours through Jesus—confidence. Not self-confidence but Holy Spirit confidence. "But as for me, I am filled with power, with the Spirit of the LORD" (Micah 3:8).

That's why I am saying it now because if I never speak it out loud, then I can never speak against it. To do this, to write these words, it terrifies me, but I have come to a place that to not do it terrifies me even more. I have come to the place that what matters to me more than my comfort and safety zone staying intact is obedience to the call of Jesus. To write is for me to be obedient. So, I'll write, staring no longer at a blank page that always seems to haunt me but only at the cross of Calvary that reminds me of the message of Jesus that pain is worth it for the sake of others. I will do this.

I joined a gym during Christmas break. I have always loved being an active person, but I usually go through these phases of intense dedication, followed by a couple weeks of, "I'll just go for a walk." However, something was different about this gym, and I have stuck with it. What was different was the people. They made me want to show up. Multiple times a week, I would make the drive down south of town to workout. Tuesday night is my favorite class.

Dripping in sweat and gulping down my last little bit of water, I always tell the girl at the front desk, "See you tomorrow," and crank up my car and head home.

Once I was home, it was dinner, shower, homework, and then the at-the-time hit TV show *This is Us.* That is how Tuesday evenings went in my world week after week. There is a room tucked away in our house that is called the white room. The all-white walls and white furniture give away where the name came from. The room used to be solely for the sake of my mom's quiet time and where she would spend her mornings in Scripture and prayer. We eventually turned it into a family room and placed a TV in there. However, what would not leave is a painting that hangs on the far-left side of the room. The painting displays the prodigal son and the father. The son who has returned wraps himself around the father's feet in humiliation, but the father is bending down to not only embrace the son but to meet him where he is at. We never talked about why we kept the painting up after remodeling the room. The Lord knew we needed that image plastered on the wall of the room that would be considered our family room, but we would also need it engraved into our hearts.

That room would still be called the white room long after the white walls were gone. There is a purity about it. It is a place where things were made right. It is a place where the prodigals truly did come home and with shame knelt down to hide their face but would be met with tears of not just the Father but by a mother, by sisters, by brothers. The white room is where both interventions took place for my brothers' drug addictions. The white room is where confessions of stealing and relapses were spoken out loud. White is a word that embodies cleansing, purity, and being made new. I truly saw that happen in that room.

Looking back, resentment that was built up, bitterness that had taken root, anger that was fuming, they all came to a halt when conversations and prayer took place in that little room. That room holds transformative moments for my family and for me personally, as well. This room is where I would sit and watch *This is Us.* Most of the episodes I watched with my hand cupped over my mouth, trying to muffle the sounds of weeping.

By the time these pages are strung together and land anywhere, especially in your hands, it is impossible to know whether *This Is Us* will even be popular anymore. So fair warning if you've never seen it: Spoiler alerts coming. The director of the show said his goal was to make viewers feel like they were watching old home videos out of order. The plot of the story includes Jack and Rebecca Pearson. They are a young married couple that is expecting triplets. Rebecca loses one of the babies in labor, but at the same time, a little boy is left at the hospital to be claimed. Jack and Rebecca take the little boy in, and they leave the hospital with Kevin, Kate, and Randall, also known as the big three.

The show takes you through their story and flips back and forth between present-day and past events. The show is tangibly showing how what happened in the past truly does affect the here and now. The climactic point of the show is when the dad, Jack Pearson, dies. For months, the show did not reveal the cause of Jack's death; we just knew that he died.

At first, I enjoyed watching the show. The creativity of the script made the writer in me giddy. They were brilliantly weaving together storylines of characters and holding intact raw emotions that come with family dynamics, especially one dealing with the aftermath of loss. After a while, episodes were regularly ending with text messages from some of my closet friends.

"Are you watching?"

"Are you okay?"

Repetitively they asked, and in my pride, I would respond with a vague answer that could tackle both questions at once and keep me safe from having to use nothing more than one word—yes. They knew before I even knew. This show, these episodes, they would snatch me backward into my own episodes. After a while, I would inevitably end up sinking into a deep depression after watching the latest episode that had aired. These episodes were serving as trigger points.

A trigger point is a sensitive area that becomes painful when compressed. Typically, it is a tender area of the body, especially of a muscle, that when stimulated gives rise to pain elsewhere in the body. This show was hitting the most tender places of my memory, even reaching the areas where I had chosen to have selective memory and was causing an array of pain to erupt. I had been a dormant volcano, and everyone around me could see the circumstances and warning signs of an eruption being likely. I, however, could not. I was living under my own expectations of who I thought I needed to be, and it was keeping me from seeing who I really was and the state I was truly in. The magma was rising through my cracks and weaknesses, just as it does through the earth's crust. The fragmented parts of my belief were becoming noticeable, and the newfound awareness of the state I was really in was being unmasked—I was angry this was my story.

With my teeth clenched, I would mumble, "This is us? No. That is me." Seeing myself in the faces of the characters, hearing myself in their dialogue, it was too much to bear. I stopped watching. I stopped watching because the moments that these characters got to share with their father were moments that I knew I would never have. Kate, the little girl, was getting everything that I had ever wanted. It was like watching someone receive the very gift you had blown out your candles and wished for every year. It is those moments when you scroll through social media and see father-daughter outings. It is the text messages you watch your friends read that their dad has sent them. It is the Father's Day commercials that are inescapable. It is everything that points you back to the fact that what most have, you don't.

However, there lies something beautiful amongst all of this. Tenderly, through the credits rolling of a TV show, what arose in me was a sincere apology.

I am sorry.

Often people don't even know that all you want to hear is just that—that they are sorry. The apology they can offer will not change the scenario. It will never serve as a dosage of medicine to relieve the pain, but it does acknowledge the pain. That is what we need sometimes, for people to acknowledge the existence of our pain. It makes you feel less crazy. It takes the confusion of your thoughts that you cannot articulate in words and make you see that those around you don't need you to try to make sense of it all for them to step in with empathy.

Some of Jesus' final words during the crucifixion were, "Father, forgive them, for they know not what they do" (Luke 23:34). The offering of an apology runs deep—deep enough to penetrate the wound and move you. Not necessarily toward healing, but toward the awareness that people see you in the middle of the fog. They see you when your vision is cloudy from tears. You might not be able to see yourself, or them, or even the Lord, but you are seen. Even in this, you are seen.

I never understood the power of offering the simple response of, "I am sorry," to someone in their circumstance until someone offered it to me. In the summer of 2018, I was back working at the camp I had worked at the previous summer, and I met a new friend who loved to write poems.

She wrote me a poem and gave it to me the night before my dad's birthday. The first two lines said, "I'm sorry. I'm sorry I don't get it." Upon reading, I felt understood for the first time. She did not get it, but I didn't need her to. When people are willing to step into the valleys with you, even the valleys you haven't even dared to give a name to yet, those are the people you want around. Her poem rekindled my own apology that I had set out to give but never ventured into. It's the apology that I want to offer to you—the one doing this thing called life without a dad. But I know that to offer it to you is to also offer it to myself.

A part of me feels selfish. How would Jesus feel about me telling myself the things I am sorrowful about? There lies the problem. My perspective of how Jesus would view my struggles, my pain, and my disappointments, was living in a realm far from the reality of what He truly thought. Who told us that Jesus would be disappointed in us if we were disappointed? Who told us that Jesus would be frustrated with our struggles? Who told us that confessing pain to Him was confessing failure? Who told us that? Who told me that?

Most of the time, I think the answer to that question is that we are the ones who told ourselves. We cannot trust ourselves. Our language that we speak is one of self, self-doubt, self-harm, self-hate, and self-protection. His language is one of truth and only truth. He is the resounding voice of truth. As He speaks, the mountains of lies that you have built your life upon crumble. He says, "Blessed are those who mourn, for they shall be comforted" (Matthew 5:4). There are things that I am disappointed with when it comes to this journey of not having an earthly father present. There are things that I am sad about. There are things that are painful. They are not things either of us has to push down beneath the surface because we think the Lord will look the other way if they come out. They are allowed to come out.

This past year, I met a high school girl though a set of God-ordained events. One of her close friends was a previous camper of mine and brought her to a worship night I had planned. I didn't know the girl at all, but I knew her story. I knew her dad had been sick for a while, and the odds weren't looking good. It felt a little awkward, especially saying it to a sixteen-year-old girl, but the night we met, I told her I had been in a similar place and if she ever wanted to talk about it that she could call. To my surprise, she reached out, and over the next couple of months, we stayed in touch.

Her dad eventually went to be with Jesus, and I will never forget her texting me after it happened. We went to dinner the very next night because she said she wanted to meet up. To sit with her in the moments following her greatest pain was an honor like I've never felt. What qualified me wasn't my mastering of grief or having all the answers for the journey she was about to embark on—it was just the fact that I had been there. We talk about how God uses our stories. I think sometimes we forget to talk about the fact that God keeps using our stories. Over and over. There is no expiration date. It has been seventeen years since losing my dad, and yet again, He allows dots to connect, paths to cross, pain to be understood, and His hope to be displayed through the simple fact that I am still here. I am still standing. There is wind in my sails and a song in my mouth, and that's enough. It communicated all that needed to be communicated sitting in a booth with a sixteen-year-old girl on a Monday night. She'll make it, and so will you.

As I drove away after attending her father's funeral, I yelled at the Lord. I told Him that I knew He would provide all that it was that she needed. I told Him I knew that He was her Father and that she would not go without. But I also told Him that I was angry that she now had to walk this road that I have been walking because doing life without your earthly father present is hard. As much as I believed and trusted Jesus for all that was to come, my heart ached for her. I was deeply sorry for what she would now have to experience. If you are sitting in the same seat that I have sat in, there is a great deal of things that I am sorry for.

I am sorry that this is what it is. I am sorry that you have had to experience the deep pain of loss. I am sorry you have had to wrestle with the "Why?" I am sorry you won't get the moments like Kate got with Jack on *This is Us.* I am sorry that you have to stare your reality in the face anytime you walk into someone's household and sit around a dinner table. I am sorry that this isn't going anywhere. I am sorry that it is permanent. I am sorry that, more often than you want, someone probably asks you to share your story. I am sorry that there are the expectations for you to know all the answers when it comes to hard things. I am sorry that everyone thinks that because someone else is experiencing a similar valley as you that you need to be connected with them. I am sorry for the things people have said about how it will all make sense someday or how everything happens for a reason. I am sorry that people will already know your story, to the extent it becomes something that doesn't even feel like yours to share, because people's shattered stories spread faster than a rumor in a high school. I am sorry that people want to all of a sudden compete to be your best friend. I am sorry there is always going to be one less person in the pictures and in the stands. I am sorry.

Listen though, there are things I am not sorry for, too. I am not sorry that you understand to treasure moments more. I am not sorry that you have had to learn to let people in, to let them meet you where you are. I am not sorry that your credibility with people leads to them being willing to listen. I am not sorry that what qualifies you to be someone to speak is not a platform that you built for yourself, nor is it the high places you have been to; it is the low places. I am not sorry that your empathy exists because of this.

Above all else, I am not sorry that you have had to learn to let Jesus catch you when you fall. I am not sorry that you have had to learn the intense level of dependency that some may never reach. I am not sorry that you have had to fight for your faith, and because of that, your faith holds firmer than some. I am sorry for what this is, but I am not sorry for who it has made you to be. I am not sorry for who this has made me to be.

Father's Day

It was June 17, 2016. Father's Day was approaching. This day, to me, is the hardest of them all because you cannot escape it. You cannot escape the reality of what isn't. The radio ads, the big events at church, the card aisle at the grocery store—everywhere you go there is a reminder of "dads," and for some of us, that is not a reminder we want. As a kid, I always signed up to go to camp during the session that started on Father's Day. It was a way for me to have something to look forward to. This day became more about, "I am going to camp!" instead of, "It's Father's Day." However, the camp days ended, and living in the real world during Father's Day was so much harder to navigate.

It was not my first time facing this day, but it was going to be Halle's. I was in the routine of spending a regular amount of time with them, and as the day got closer, we started to have a pretty vague conversation about it. I didn't know how much Halle understood or how much to say. But, she told me that she didn't want to go to church because she didn't want to do the craft that she knew they would have you make to give to your dad. She did not want to have to tell her teacher that she didn't have a dad to give it to. She summed up how so many of us feel on this day. We do not want to face the reality of what we don't have. For years, I could escape it. That is what camp did for me. However, now, when Father's Day approaches and camp is no more, it has become unavoidable.

I was eighteen. It was a Thursday afternoon. I was picking up more babysitting gigs to make a little extra money. I made the drive to the city to babysit, something I was doing two or three times a week, at this point. What was usually episodes of Curious George and toy trucks turned into, "Can we do a craft for Father's Day?" You see, I was already struggling. As hard as it is for me to admit that, I was. Every year the week of Father's Day rolls around, and I go into this funk. I become so unresponsive, unreceptive, and uninterested in almost anything. I grow numb. It lasts a couple days, and then I am fine, but it happens, and I never say anything to anybody. When two kids ask you to help them make a Father's Day present, it is a painful shot to a wound that has already been ripped wide open.

I am learning to be honest. Honest not only to whoever might read this but honest with myself. Somewhere along the way, I adopted this visual in my head: I am standing at a stop sign, and to the left is the road named, "I am okay," and to the right is the road, "I am not okay." There is no middle ground; I have to choose, and once I do, I tell myself that I have to stay on that road. I tell myself that it's a one-way, and you can't ever go the other way. Balance is not a trait I possess.

When a six-year-old little boy asked me to help him make a card for his dad, it hurt. For too long, people have made this bold assertion that time heals things. I do not believe that. Jesus heals things, and the concept of time does not apply to Jesus. It is not time that we need, it is Him. Yet, I found myself staring at my reflection in the mirror, saying, "You have done this before. Be okay." When I start falling into the thought of, "Maybe I am not okay," I let myself believe the lie that since so much time has passed, if I were to tell people I am struggling they will think I am just doing it for sympathy, or for attention.

I create these expectations for myself that people need me to talk about the goodness of the Lord on the days that are obviously hard. Which do not get me wrong, Jesus is still good. I still believe that, but it does not negate the fact that sometimes you want to wish away the moment you are in. It does not negate the fact that no matter how much time has passed, you can wake up in the morning wishing it could all be undone. It does not negate the fact that although Jesus so faithfully lets drops of healing rain fall down on you that you still have moments when it hurts.

I have gotten it wrong. You do not have to choose a road. You do not have to be one extreme or the other. You do not have to be fresh off a loss, whatever form that loss might be, to have the right to struggle. Loss breaks you. Jesus pieces the broken things back together, takes the ashes, and transforms them into beauty. But loss also leaves an imprint on you. The things that imprint us affect us not just in that moment but forever. You can be okay one second and not okay the next. You can be spiritually growing, in the Word, and actively pursuing the Lord, and there is still freedom for you to stop, to say to yourself that it hurts, and to say to a hurting world that they are allowed to hurt. You can go to the same place you have been before. You can go there again.

"...at this they wept aloud again" (Ruth 1:14). They wept again. It doesn't matter if it is year twenty, and you find yourself sitting in your car with tears streaming down your face. It doesn't matter if it is a normal day, and you just have a moment. You have the complete freedom to weep, and then to weep again. Naomi and her daughter-in-law Ruth had experienced great loss in the death of both their husbands. Though there was weeping, the direction in which they wept is what truly matters. Ruth and Naomi wept, but they wept forward. They stopped to weep, but then they kept going. You do not have to choose only one road to walk down. You can be not okay, or you can be okay, but you have to keep putting one foot in front of the other. You cannot let the weeping stop you. Do not let it stop you from continuing to pursue the Lord.

I babysit so often for some families that when I am there, I have caught on and can tell what the baby's cry means. I know when it's a fake cry. I know when it's a, "I want more food," cry. I know when it's a, "Pick me up," cry. I started thinking about the fact that a parent knows their child's cry way better than a babysitter does. A father knows his child's cry. That is the thought that I pound into my heart on Father's Day. The thought that I still have a Father who hears me. A Father who sees my tears and hears them. A Father who knows exactly what they mean and knows exactly what I need.

He will turn your mourning into dancing, but He allows you to step off the dance floor. But know, He never stops playing the music. Tune back in when you are ready. Today, cry all the tears, wipe them, feel them, but don't let them stop you. It is possible to cry and walk at the same time. Walk straight down whatever road you need to be on today. Jesus will meet you right where you are. If you need to, take a little break from dancing, but when tomorrow comes, put those shoes on and get back out there. There is always a song playing over you. It is the perfect Father singing a lullaby over His child.

This day is a liar. I had to learn that. My dad might not be here, but I can still celebrate him and his life. Your dad might not be here, but you can still celebrate him. Maybe you don't think your dad is one worth celebrating. I know too many girls that feel this way. Jesus fills in the gaps. Maybe it is your uncle, your grandfather, your older brother, a friend's dad. We all have someone that has taken that father figure role in our life. Celebrate them today. You can celebrate someone today. You can celebrate and feel the pain all at the same time.

I attended a women's Bible study one night when the passage we were studying was Psalm 119. While the woman was teaching on this passage, she briefly mentioned Psalm 126, and the words of that chapter grabbed my attention. I had never read Psalm 126, but I went home to read it and then even memorized it that night. In the days following, I would recite it over and over and over. When I couldn't sleep, I would say it. When I drove, I would play it out loud from my phone. It became my soundtrack. You need something playing over you when darkness is hovering. Psalm 126 became that for me.

I have kept digging into Psalm 126, and I know that days like Father's Day, or your loved one's birthday, can be days wrapped in bright lights and cheer, making those who have great pain feel it in a deeper way. Psalm 126 is simply the message that tearful sowing will one day end in joyful singing. The words of Psalm 126 have been for me a reminder to my soul that sometimes aches. They have been a weapon to push back the darkness and a reminder that my pain is not meaningless.

Psalms 120-134 are a collection of chapters from the book of Psalms called "Song of Ascents." These are thought to be the songs the pilgrims would sing as they ascended into Jerusalem for one of the three main annual Jewish Festivals. God's law required males to go to Jerusalem for three sacred festivals or feasts: the Feast of Unleavened Bread, the Feast of Weeks, and the Feast of Booths (Deut. 16:16). When the people would make the journey to Jerusalem, these are the songs they would sing along the way. Psalm 126 is a part of those songs.

"When the Lord restored the fortunes of Zion, we were like those who dream" (Psalm 126:1). The opening verse of this chapter is referencing the return of the Jewish community from exile in Babylon. King Cyrus had decreed they could return to their home in Jerusalem (Ezra 1:1-11). I am sure that many of the Jews, while in captivity, doubted they would ever experience freedom again. I am sure they doubted they would ever return to their homeland, but they would not let themselves forget Jerusalem.

> By the waters of Babylon, there we sat down and wept, when we remembered Zion. On the willows there we hung up our lyres. For there our captors required of us songs, and our tormentors, mirth, saying, "Sing us one of the songs of Zion!" How shall we sing the Lord's song in a foreign land? If I forget you, O Jerusalem, let my right hand forget its skill! Let my tongue stick to the roof of my mouth, if I do not remember you, if I do not set Jerusalem above my highest joy! (Psalm 137: 1-6)

They would sit by the river, weeping, praying, and remembering. They did not want to forget. They begged of Him, "Don't let us forget, Lord."

Too many of us are sitting by a river, in a foreign land, that God never meant for us to live in, and we are forgetting. We are sitting by the river of our failures, fears, and shortcomings. Some of us are sitting next to the river of anxiety and depression. We are sitting by a river, just as the Jewish people did, but we are not doing as they did. We must weep. We must pray. We must express that we recognize that where we are is not where we are meant to be. It was the unsettledness and awareness in them that Babylon was not the land they wanted to settle in that brought forth desperate prayers for the Lord to change the scenery. Do not settle for living by a river, in a land that you know God does not intend for you to live in. Do not settle for accepting that you have lived next to that river for too long to leave it.

"...we were like those who dream" (Psalm 126:1). Dreams in the Old Testament often served as vehicles to redemption. Joseph saved his family from famine because of a dream. Daniel attained his position through the dreams of Nebuchadnezzar. Jacob received the promises of God for his people and himself through a dream. Solomon got the chance to ask for wisdom in a dream where the Lord appeared to him. I can't help but think that when the Psalmist said, "We were like those who dream," it was a reference to those who were blessed by a dream the Lord let them experience. The restoration in Zion was the vehicle to the Jewish peoples' redemption. The Psalmist was saying that their return home was a dream. Dreams can be vehicles to redemption. A synonym for the word redemption is recovery.

The effects of pain, loss, heartache, and struggle leave a wound. A wound that needs to recover. A dream could pave the way to a recovery of your wound. Let yourself dream. Joseph was known for being a slave, but Joseph was also known for being a dreamer. The messy part of your story does not have to be the only thing you are known for. That struggle of yours does not have to be the only thing you are known for. You are not enslaved to it. Weep. Move forward. Celebrate. Remember. Dream. Do all of this, but if the moment comes and you need a breather, take a break from dancing. I usually do on Father's Day.

Novembers

Thanksgiving. It's accompanied by football, flannels, and the crisp fall air. It rolls around once a year, and we celebrate a week off from school and the shopping deals that are to come Friday morning. We go around the table and answer our mom's question of, "What are you thankful for?" with such ease. Our Instagram post captions get a little longer as we unravel how thankful we are for _____ (you fill in the blank). We beam with joy and pride ourselves in the heart of gratitude we always seem to be able to cultivate on a Thursday in November. It is harder for those of us in the midst of heartbreak, though. The holidays are supposed to be the most wonderful time of the year, but for others, it only intensifies missing people.

I don't want to pass over this month. November is the month when gratitude is the banner hovering over all of us. Yet, November is the month that my deepest loss occurred. As the "give thanks" signs start to make their way into homes, the temptation to become resentful and angry surfaces in my heart. I look back and think to myself, "You made it this far." I look forward and see how much life is still ahead.

The moments that he will miss will only increase. There have been so many journal entries scribbled with words that have aimed to do their best to describe what was felt, yet somehow, no words have ever actually been able to articulate it. The harsh reality that I am sitting in is that there are still more blank journal pages to be filled. There are still many moments that he will miss. The happy moments will forever be accompanied by a sense of sadness because he won't be here.

Sometimes November rolls around, and the temptation to be angry really isn't a temptation at all. Then I feel guilty. Or November rolls around, and for so long, I have lived under the presumed expectations of how I am supposed to feel that I have no idea how to untangle what really does exist. Especially in the world of social media, where we feel as if people are watching with a front-row seat to our grief process, and because of that, we believe we must always preserve our image.

Loss does not come with the responsibility to always have the right words to say. Loss does not come with the responsibility to post something on the hardest day of the year, with beautiful words strung together that will inspire. Loss does not come with the responsibility to feel a certain way after a certain amount of time. Loss does not come with the responsibility to "share your story" every time someone asks. Grief was never meant to be attractive. Grief was never meant for you to leverage it for followers.

Grief is about you and God getting in the trenches together, and when you come out of that trench, then it will be time to speak of how God was present even there. What I see happening is that people are coming out of the trenches before it is time, or people are never going into the trenches at all. This leaves us with too many people feeling the pressure to "say something," and the words that manifest lack vulnerability and sincerity because they do not possess raw emotion.

You cannot speak about that which you have not truly dared to experience. I am preaching at myself here. November 21 rolls around every year, and I have a perfectly written Instagram caption that will tug at the heartstrings of my followers, but what I have come to realize is that I have written about November 21 many times yet have not lived it. There are a lot of us out there. Those of us who have written but haven't really lived it.

What does it mean to live and not just write? It means being okay with sitting in the tension for a little while. It means to be okay with slipping away into the secret place and going unseen. It means to wrestle with God and work through doubts, questions, and anger. It means to not post. It means to know that you can be silent. It means to figure out how you really feel and to show it. It means to let your life speak louder than your words ever could. It means to stop putting so much pressure on yourself.

November—you usually come with so many "shoulds" or "should nots," and I lose myself completely. You usually come with words that lack emotion because of a strong willpower to avoid all emotion. Sometimes you come with a slight case of depression and exhaustion. Sometimes you come with a retreat mentality, and from even my closest friends I shut the door. You don't even need to come with a mask because I've become pretty good at making my own façade over the years. You always come with a cry from my soul saying, "I miss him," but sometimes that cry never endures the journey to become an audible whisper. Deep down, I know that November will always be accompanied by a wish for the story to not be what it is, and it is about time that I come to terms with that.

Until I give myself permission to still miss him, I will never be able to give someone else the permission. I will never be able to speak on what I am not living. I will never take someone somewhere I have not been myself. Oh, how I want us to live through the grief and not just write about it. Oh, how I want us to not say anything sometimes. Oh, how I want more people to go to the trenches so they can one day rise up singing a song that actually means something.

> I waited patiently for the LORD; he inclined to me and heard my cry. He drew me up from the pit of destruction, out of the miry bog, and set my feet upon a rock, making my steps secure. He put a new song in my mouth, a song of praise to our God. Many will see and fear, and put their trust in the LORD (Psalm 40: 1-3).

David said the Lord lifted Him out of the pit and put a new song in his mouth. There are a lot of people out there singing songs about how to deal with the hard times, and the thing is we don't need any more people singing the same songs. We need people singing new songs. We need people to get in the trenches and then let the Lord set their feet on a firm place to stand. You can go there, my friend. You can disappear from the public eye for a split second. You can let it be you and God so that one day you can tell your story. The real story, not just the story you have become good at telling. We want real. We want mud and mire. We want a new song.

I have had moments when my song has had a change in tune. A couple words here and there have started to change as I have gone back and started to deal with the loss of my dad, but I want a completely new song. It's the month of gratitude, and it's a fight to cultivate that spirit. However, when I look back at these last seventeen years, in one hand, I see the messy, painful, and broken moments. In the other hand, I see the truth of who God is and His promises. When the two collide, they simply paint the picture of the cross—tragedy and triumph.

That's what these years have been—tragedy yet triumph. I cannot help but be thankful for a God who takes complete opposites and works them together for a purpose far greater than we could ever imagine. Maybe things would be easier if my life had been all triumph and no tragedy. But my story is one where every ounce of heartache is leading up to a, "But God." A story where I will never minimize the pain, but I will also always maximize who Jesus is and what He has done.

Don't you see it? Those moments in the trenches are building up to that, "But God" declaration. The more descriptive, honest, and vulnerable you can be, the more intensified and amplified that moment will be. The tragedy is not the climax of the story, the triumph is. The tragedy is the rising action, which always leads to the climax. The climax centers on a person. The person is not you, it's Jesus. Let the tragedy be known. Let the trenches be a real place you have been. Let there be a new song. Let the song always declare the triumph.

We are all trying to land on the idea of gratitude as Thanksgiving rolls around. We are trying to be people who are thankful, but it is important that we look not to our Instagram feeds for how to be people of gratitude. We must look to Scripture to see what Jesus has to say about giving thanks. He spoke the oceans into existence and gave them firm borders of how far they were allowed to come. He spun the galaxies into motion and threw the stars into the blank sky, naming every one of them. Yet, when Jesus came to earth, He set a beautiful example for us of what it means to give thanks. The One who provides all that we need and created all that there is, took time to continuously thank the Father.

For us who look to Him, that says, "It matters." The Son of God never does anything that does not have the utmost importance, and He never asks of us something He hasn't already set the example for. We can know that He wants us to have this spirit of giving thanks, but we can take a deep breath because we don't have to figure this out on our own. He has shown us what it looks like.

> "he took the seven loaves and the fish, and having given thanks he broke them and gave them to the disciples, and the disciples gave them to the crowds" (Matthew 15:36).

> "Jesus said to her, 'Did I not tell you that if you believed you would see the glory of God?' So they took away the stone. And Jesus lifted up his eyes and said, "Father, I thank you that you have heard me. I knew that you always hear me, but I said this on account of the people standing around, that they may believe that you sent me"' (John 11:40-42).

When Jesus gave thanks, great things followed. He gave thanks for the bread and fish when the feeding of the five thousand happened. He gave thanks for the fact God heard His prayer, and His dear friend Lazarus rose from the dead.

One of the most significant times that Jesus gave thanks was before the Passover meal. "While they were eating, Jesus took bread, and when he had given thanks, he broke it and gave it to his disciples, saying, 'Take and eat; this is my body'" (Matthew 26:26 NIV). He sat around a table, surrounded by His disciples, knowing that in a short time, He would be nailed to the cross. He was aware of the suffering that was about to take place, and what did He do? He stood up in front of a room full of people and gave thanks. When Jesus gave thanks, great things followed. In this case, what was to follow was the spotless Lamb being slain, bringing our redemption.

Jesus showed us that giving thanks is something we have over complicated. If you are looking for an equation of how to reach this spirit of thanksgiving, Jesus has given it. You pause. You acknowledge the fact that everything we receive comes from God and God alone. Acknowledging that should produce praise in you. Pause + Praise = Thanksgiving.

"Give thanks in all circumstances" (1 Thessalonians 5:18). In all circumstances—in joy and in sorrow. It's times like the holiday seasons that being thankful seems unobtainable. It seems impossible. It seems as if there is no way it can be written on the fabric of our hearts. That is exactly what Satan wants you to believe. The enemy will take your feelings and let them speak louder than the truth. Your feelings are valid. However, your feelings are not the deciding factor.

My mom tells us the story often about when a family friend stood in the doorway of our home after my father died and said, "The only way your children will ever get through this is by choosing gratitude." I think I am finally starting to understand what she meant. Gratitude is the weapon that constantly defeats Satan. He arrives on the scene, trying to draw up a scheme to make us falter in our belief, but gratitude shuts Satan down before the blueprints of his plan are even put into action. Gratitude looks past what isn't and finds what is.

Today, we must make a choice. We have this command to give thanks in all circumstances, and we have to fight for it to be true of us. We have the example Jesus gave us to give thanks even knowing what was to happen to Him. I think Jesus knew that in order for the praise to come, at times, there has to be a pause. Maybe today, you have to pause a little longer to find something you are thankful for. Maybe you have to pick your brain and dig deep. Sit in the pause because the pause will produce praise at some point. The wind in your hair, the toothpaste on your toothbrush, the light you are reading these words under right now, big or small, it doesn't matter but find something.

This does not diminish your pain. It does not change your story. It does not bring instant healing. What it does is it changes your perspective entirely. It gives you a new mindset. The mindset that says: I will look at what I do have and not just what I don't. And when your eyes can't seem to see it and your lips can't seem to mutter a, "Thank you," His grace meets you right where you are, and His Holy Spirit will intercede on your behalf.

"Likewise the Spirit helps us in our weakness. For we do not know what to pray for as we ought, but the Spirit himself intercedes for us with groanings too deep for words" (Romans 8:26).

If the gratitude is not there, ask Him to get you there. Our circumstances often block us from seeing anything else. Challenge yourself to look beyond the very thing that is diminishing your spirit of thanksgiving. The odds are there is, in fact, something good in this story of yours, you might just be missing it. Choose it. Choose gratitude even when it makes no sense at all because gratitude always wins. Even with empty chairs at the dinner table and family pictures hanging in living rooms that don't match what you are looking at now, the people of God can't settle for anything less than to have a heart that matches what the Lord is asking of us—to give thanks.

Thanksgiving is more than just a holiday. It is more than just saying what we're thankful for. It is more than a feeling. It is a spirit we must have. It is a choice we must make. It is an example that Jesus set for us. How do we keep this up? When November comes to an end, that doesn't mean we zoom out on the idea of gratitude. We can zoom in even more. November is ending, but December is coming with another holiday. We need to get it now, so it lasts.

Usually, the anniversary of my father's death falls very close to Thanksgiving. It was our first holiday without him. We always had a house full of people, and we invited all to the table to eat. There is another table we are being invited to today, though. The table is not filled with a feast. Jesus works differently than we do. We think we need it all, and we need it all right now. In fear, we look to the days ahead and worry about how we will get what we need. We go into survival mode and start behaving as if we only have a certain amount of time to obtain fuel for the days to come. I love that He is the God of the daily bread. He does not operate on our time, yet in His kindness, He steps into our time frame and gives what we need on a daily basis.

When the Israelites wandered in the wilderness, they went into that same frantic state we go into sometimes. They saw the journey ahead, and they doubted that God would provide what they needed, but the Lord spoke a word to Moses. "Then the LORD said to Moses, "Behold, I am about to rain bread from heaven for you, and the people shall go out and gather a day's portion every day, that I may test them, whether they will walk in my law or not" (Exodus 16:4).

Go out and gather enough for that day. God gives what we need for the day. He sustains, and He provides. He does not give us anything more or anything less. Not only does He give, but He gives and meets our exact needs. He sees us. He sees you. This is a truth you can build your life on: God gives us what we need on a daily basis, so if you don't have it today, you don't need it for today. My mom would tell us all the time that we had my dad for the exact amount of time we needed to have him. Those words might land more painfully for those of you fresh into a loss, but they are true. He isn't a God who makes mistakes, and your story is not the exception.

Many of us have prayed the Lord's Prayer a million times, not realizing that one of the lines is a primary way to ensure we never lose this spirit of Thanksgiving. "Give us this day our daily bread" (Matthew 6:11). To pray that prayer is to submit to Jesus. It is to confess that we believe He knows our needs better than we do. If we can realize that He is the God of the daily bread, we will see that at the end of every day, we have been given all that we need. He gives us our daily bread, and daily we must thank Him. November 21 is not an exception to that. At the end of the day that reminds me deeply of my father's death, I can lay my head down at night, knowing that all that I needed for that day was provided. I can offer up my thanks.

We started a tradition years ago on Thanksgiving day where everyone in my family and my extended family circle around in our living room. We have a candle sitting on the wooden table, and we light it to remember everyone who is not with us. My mom asks that we take a moment of silence. I think it is her way of protecting us from never thinking we have to skip over it. We look down at the ground. We pause, and then we praise. The transition from the moment of silence into prayer is the movement of looking up. You were moments ago looking down, where all you see is the rug below your feet, but the shift in your gaze allows you to look up at everything and everyone that is around you.

That is the movement we have to make today. Look up. Raise your chin. Don't keep looking at the rocky ground beneath your feet. If your eyes could find their way to what is around you, your heart could find the motivation to fight to have a song of thanksgiving rise from within you. It would be a shame to stay in the belief that He is just a God who takes. He gives. He gives daily. He gives just what we need. For that, and because of that, we always have a reason to say, "Thank you."

The Conversation

Tuesdays. Around where I live, they are trash days. No, really, the trash men come on Tuesdays. Other than that, there is not really anything special about them. They aren't Mondays. They don't come with a dreaded start of another work week. For us ladies, they aren't accompanied by Chris Harrison, cheese plates, and another episode of The Bachelor. They aren't like Wednesdays who have an alter ego called "hump day." They don't let you rejoice like Thursdays do because it is almost the weekend. Lastly, they surely aren't Fridays. Fridays are paired with shouts of victories because you made it through another week. Tuesdays, well, they are just Tuesdays. This Tuesday was more than that, though.

The fall air had finally made its way to Atlanta. The slight breeze meant it was cool enough for me to wear long sleeves. I had bought a shirt a month before that I was obsessed with. At the time, it didn't make sense to buy it. It was still hot outside. As any girl would, I bought the shirt anyway. That is why I remember what I had on so clearly because I had waited to wear it. I did not know that in the days to come, that shirt would be a reminder of a defeat.

I sat in my living room with a couple of friends. Four, to be exact. One girl and three guys. One of the guys was in his first semester of seminary and had a paper due that night. My friend made a joke about him asking my advice on the paper. She said, "Ask the expert in the room. She is writing a book." I knew what was coming next. Two of the guys were new friends. They didn't know about the book, and they most definitely didn't know my story.

What followed was the million-dollar question: What is the book about? I have fought long and hard to believe in what these words are. I am confident in an anointing the Lord has coated these pages with. However, in this moment, I did not want to answer the question. It dawned on me that up until this point, everyone that knew what this book was going to be was someone that already knew my story. I hesitated to speak and even tried to change the conversation because I did not want to have this conversation. Not here. Not now. Not when I wasn't prepared. Not when I thought it was too soon.

It is a conversation we are always going to have. The conversation that lets someone in on the reality of our absent father. Whether it be from loss, divorce, or even emotionally unavailable, there will always come a time when we have to let people in on that side of the story. For those of us who have experienced loss, we all have that one part of our story. When this moment comes, and the conversation starts to unfold, the enemy will use it as a test against you. He will pose the question, "Do you really believe they aren't going to see you differently after they know this?" I have spent the last seventeen years fighting to not identify myself as fatherless. However, what I have come to see is that if we are not careful, we might not let it give us our identity, but we will still believe the lie that it has stained our identity. That is what I have done.

We can take drastic measures to protect ourselves and even pray in preparation when we know the time is coming for us to let someone new in. We can choose when the conversation is supposed to happen. Yet, what do we do when it comes without planning? It is the unexpected moments when you have to let someone in that will reveal how firm your stake is in the identity Christ gives you. I rolled off the answer to the question about the book in such a desensitized way. The approach I took was that of a high school student answering a short answer question—I gave the bare minimum. I gave them enough, and then I changed the topic.

The night went on, but I couldn't shake the fact that these two new friends now knew the most broken part of my story. I was sad. The problem wasn't that I was sad about the story itself. The problem was that I was sad that I had to tell them and that they had to know.

My foundation was revealed that night. I saw my absent father as an added burden to anyone that knew me or would come to know me. I had confidence in who Jesus said I was, but I was still not letting go of the belief that the loss of my father affected who I was. The enemy wants nothing more for those of us with absent fathers than to believe that we are our own kind of brand, different from the rest of the world. What happens sometimes is that we let ourselves go too far in our thinking and believe that parts of our stories have marked us so severely that they have created a disability and added responsibility to those around us. It is not true.

"Behold, like the clay in the potter's hand, so are you in my hand, O house of Israel" (Jeremiah 18:6). What the Lord does as the potter is take you in His hands and mold you. He continuously lets His hands smooth over the places that keep resurfacing with false beliefs about who you are and what you think people see you as. As followers of Jesus, we don't get to reach the point where we finally let Him rip the name tag off our shirt only for us to believe there is a residue still there. You are not stained. You are a new creation. The old has gone, and the new has come. Jesus has let go of the old. There comes a time when we must let go of it too. For most of us, the old category that is the last to go is our thinking. We have to start thinking in a new way about ourselves.

The conversation is going to happen, and then it is going to happen again. We will never stop dreading these moments until we anchor ourselves to new thinking. New thinking is this:

I am not a burden; I am beloved.

I am not disabled; I am a daughter.

I am not stained; I am a saint.

I think about John 12, where it talks about the unbelief among the Jews. Jesus had performed many signs and wonders, and there were still those who didn't believe. I don't want us to be the kind of people who have seen who Jesus is and know what He has done and still doubt the truth of who He says we are. I want us to believe Him when He tells us that we are no longer slaves. That includes being a slave to our wrong beliefs about our identity. I want us to believe Him when He calls us children and heirs (Galatians 4:7).

The reality is on that Tuesday night, in that living room, I shackled myself back to my old thinking. Jesus has completely and totally set me free from all labels this world and I can put on myself. This was my own doing. This was me not taking Him at His word. This was my belief slipping. My belief was slipping because fear was rising. At the root, anytime the conversation is about to happen where I have to tell someone about the broken parts of my story, often there is a part of me that is afraid of how people will respond. Fear will always stop your belief.

"Yet at the same time many even among the leaders believed in him. But because of the Pharisees they would not openly acknowledge their faith for fear they would be put out of the synagogue;" (John 12:42 NIV). The people would not acknowledge their belief because of their fear. I lost sight of my belief because of my fear. My foundation has to be firmer. My belief has to hold tighter. As much as I wish that on that Tuesday night I didn't have to stare face to face with my unstable foundation, I am thankful that I did. Now I know that in order for me to withstand these moments, I have to go back to the Potter's wheel. I have to lay myself down there and tell the Potter that I need Him to smooth out the places where I am getting it wrong again.

The conversation will have to happen. My hope for you and for me isn't that we find more ways to avoid it or to deflect the feelings that come with it. My hope is that we would be so secure in who the Lord says we are that we will know that letting people in on the story doesn't have to feel like airing our dirty laundry. It doesn't have to feel like we are handing them our baggage. We are handing them a part of our testimony. We are handing them a storyline that says we are overcomers. We are handing them the work of Christ in our life. When we look at it that way, we won't dread the conversation, we will delight in it. All of this will hinge on one thing, though. Will we let go of our old thinking and welcome the new?

Have you ever noticed that if you are outside when it starts raining, you don't stop moving? If anything, you quicken your step. You pick up the speed. The harder it rains, the faster you run to your intended destination. When you arrive, yes, there will be remnants of the rain on your clothing. People will know. They will ask fewer questions than you think. How you got there, what you walked through to get there, no, that won't be what captivates them. It will simply be the fact you arrived. You made it.

"I made it." Sometimes that is all you need to let the story be. Sometimes that is all the people around you need the story to be. "I made it," does away with a tidy faith. No one who had to fight for anything arrived into the banqueting hall with polished armor that wasn't damaged. Their armor might have been damaged, but they were not. He offers us an armor for this life we live. We are protected. We might arrive out of breath and with a sweaty forehead, but then we kneel before the King and get to say, "Here I am. I made it."

This journey on its own isn't something worth fighting for. But kneeling before the King and getting to say, "I made it;" that makes the journey a fight I am not willing to ever forfeit. If this is going to be a battlefield I am on every day, then I actually want the rain. It soothes the wounds. Even the rain, Jesus can take and use for my good. The conversation doesn't have to be what you think it has to be. It can simply be: This is what I made it through. Because you are making it.

Put Me in Coach

My father was a sports fanatic. He was the kind of dad that would get thrown out of a church league basketball game because everything was treated like you were competing for an Olympic medal. I know without a doubt where I got my competitive side. Growing up, my oldest brother was always the athlete of the family. His baseball team traveled all over the place, playing in different tournaments. His trophies collected dust in the basement for years until my mom told him he had to do something with them. They didn't mean as much to him as he got older, so he ended up tossing them. My brother didn't need the trophies, he had the memories. They would outlast any piece of metal.

Spending a Saturday afternoon at a baseball field was not out of the ordinary for me. My mom would send me with dad to all the games. I guess it was a way to get one more kid out of the house for the day. I would sit in the stands with our family friends and watch inning after inning. I grew up watching my brother play baseball, but I also grew up watching my dad coach him. After my dad died, my brother never picked up a baseball again.

All this time, I have been wrestling with "what could have been," and I so often forget that my older siblings have their own wrestling match. Theirs is much different than mine. Theirs is with what was. My brother couldn't bear to stand on a field and look over to third base where a man stood that was not who it was before. Baseball was his and my dad's thing. It was two-fold. There would be no baseball if there was no dad. He put the glove down and never picked it back up again.

When it came time for me to make my debut in the sports world, it came with stomach aches and bad cases of anxiety. Before rec basketball games you would know where to find me. I would hide in the bathroom until my mom would come talk me out of the stall. Before softball games I would complain that I thought I was going to be sick the whole car ride there. Looking back now, I can see that I was terrified. I thought there was only room for one athlete in our family. We could only have one athlete, and that spot was already taken. My brother was the one my dad invested so much time in when it came to sports. How was I going to try to get off the sideline into a game when I didn't have the same coach he did? I believed the lie that to be a young girl without a father in the stands would make me stand out too much. I did not have what it took.

We all want a coach. A person to tell us how we can be better. We want the person standing at third base, championing us on to keep running. We want the high five telling us we did good. We all want a coach, and I wanted the same chance to experience my dad being the coach as my brother did, but I was never going to get that. The understanding of this came with me pushing down my obsession with all things sports. I wouldn't be the girl who showed up to every practice with her mom when I knew that almost everyone else would be arriving with their dads. If their dad wasn't the coach, he would surely stay and watch the entire practice. My mom had five other kids. She didn't really understand sports, nor did she have the capacity to sit through two-hour practices. Sporting events became a time when I was very much surrounded by people but had never felt so alone.

That first season playing on a competitive softball team was where it all started. I loved sports. I loved the game. There was no way I could not play. We won some type of something that season. Maybe a participation medal, because we all won those back in the days. Whatever it is, it was my first. It was my first accolade in the sports world. I didn't keep it, though. I left it somewhere pretty special.

It was one of the few rare visits I made to Dad's gravesite over the years. I asked my mom if she could take me. There is a spot for flowers on my dad's headstone—a vase. I took the flowers out and placed the medal around it and slid it down. I put the flowers back where they belonged, and I left it there. I am sure it got rusted over the years. I am sure the rain did damage to it. But I knew that is where I wanted it to be.

It was my way of telling my dad that there was more than one athlete in this family and that my brother wasn't the only one who got that side of him. It was my way of telling him that I had done it. I had wished I could have done it with him. I had wished he could have stood at the fence and watched. But I had still done it, and I had a medal to prove it. It was the mark of competing for a season, but really it was the start of me telling myself that a girl without a father has every right to play the sports she loves just like anyone else.

I played softball for years. I did the whole traveling thing. The roles changed. What my brother once did, I was now doing. My mom came to as many games as she could, but Coach Sam (yep, the same Coach Sam you have heard me talk about before) became my personal Uber and became a person my mom knew she could trust to send me with to play. It was kind of the Lord to let the person who did become my coach be someone that grew up playing sports with my dad. He wasn't my dad. I still wasn't getting to experience that, but the Lord was letting me get just about as close to it as I could. Jesus does that. He is always letting us be closer than we know to the things we think are so far away. We often question His proximity to us, and yet He is always closer than we know.

The long hot days got old to me really fast. I made the switch to volleyball in middle school and never looked back. Just as with softball, I did the whole nine yards. I played for my school team during the fall and started traveling for tournament play as soon as the school season was over. I have loved few things as much as I loved volleyball. From sixth grade until I graduated high school, I spent every waking and breathing second in the gym.

My junior year, I thought about going back to play softball for the season. Volleyball and softball both happened during the fall, or I would have played both. Our school volleyball team wasn't looking to be very good, and I am that kind of player who really hates to lose. I thought my chances at a more enjoyable season would be on the field instead of on the court.

I got a text from a girl who was a year older than me, who played volleyball as well. In short, she put it all out there that they were going to be desperate for players and begged me to reconsider. I gave in and went to practice. The school I went to was so tiny that we didn't need to have tryouts. You knew whether you would play or not. There was a scheduling conflict, and we ended up having to relocate to a nearby gym for our first practice. We practiced. All nine of us. Things didn't look good. We were small in numbers compared to every other team. The only thing we had going for us was that small also meant closely knit.

The first game of the season arrived, and we lost. Our star player, who went on to play D1 volleyball, twisted her ankle. The season was over, and it had just started. We always do that, don't we? Decide how the end is going to play out based on the beginning when we know that God has never let the beginning of a story dictate the ending of the story. The people of Israel watched the Messiah hang on a cross. I am sure they had decided how the story was going to go, but we don't decide how the story goes. The most unexpected ending came because Jesus is in the business of writing endings that are thrilling and what we never believed could have happened. Victory can still come despite the taste of defeat coming every now and then.

Call it a Cinderella season, call it a comeback, call it the underdog story, call it whatever you want to, but that volleyball season did not go the way any of us thought it would. Soon, every player was back in good health, and things started clicking. We started winning and then winning some more. Then we started beating teams that we never expected to even stand a chance with. We realized slowly but surely that we had more potential than we thought. Our coach sat us down one day after practice and told us that if we wanted it, we had what it took to win the state championship. There's that coach again, doing what we all want, telling us that we have what it takes if we will fight for it.

With such a small team, it meant that there were no chances for players to rest and recover. It was taking a toll on all of us, but especially me. My shoulder started bothering me halfway through the season, and I complained about it to my mom. As she always does, she told me to go for a run and drink some water. Those were her problem-solvers for everything. That and Vick's Vaporub. I kept playing until the pain was getting to the point of being unbearable. I was struggling to even serve without feeling like my shoulder might detach from my body.

My coach was an ER doctor and had picked up on the pain I was in. I hadn't told him or anyone else for that matter. I didn't want them to know. I thought if they knew, then they would take me out of the game. They would see me as the weak link. When he questioned me about it, I denied it. He asked me to go to the back line and serve. One toss and just extending my arm up in preparation to serve, and he already knew. I couldn't even bear to hit it. I thought he was going to be furious, disappointed in me. His response was the complete opposite. He said, "Let's go get this looked at." He took me to a physical therapist that was a friend of his.

There is something to learn here. Being in pain doesn't mean that you have to be out of the game. It doesn't mean that you are going to get benched and be considered the weak link. Pain doesn't have to be hidden from those around us. Sometimes the people around you can help in ways that you are prohibiting them from doing because, in your shame, you are staying silent. Let people take you where you might not be able to go to yourself. Let them be the driver of the car and navigate you to a place where you might just find healing. Sometimes we can't drive ourselves. That's okay. It is why God gave us people.

It didn't take long for the doctor to know what the problem was. I had torn my labrum in my shoulder. The labrum is a piece of fibrocartilage, which is rubbery tissue, that is attached to the rim of the shoulder socket that helps keep the ball of the joint in place. The doctor explained it to me this way—the labrum is what holds all of the muscles together. When I explained that we were about to head into the state playoffs soon and there was not a shot that I was going to sit them out, he recommended some different exercises to strengthen my shoulder and muscle manipulation to help relieve some of the pressure. Basically, he gave me some options to allow me to just make it through. I would have temporary relief. I would do the bare minimum. I would sub in during my rotation and sub out and immediately start icing. It was the farthest thing from ideal, but it was enough to make it through the games.

We made it to the state championship that year. A miracle season indeed. Our opponent was the same school that we lost to at the beginning of the season. It was a reminder to me that we get a shot to stand face to face with things that defeated us before. Typically matches are played best two out of three, but in a game with this much at stake, you play three out of five. The first four games are played to twenty-five, and you have to win by two points. The fifth game, if needed, is only played to fifteen. Those were some of the longest games of my life. We won, and they won. We won, and they won. In every game, there was a two-point difference, and neither side was backing down. We were exhausted, but we had to go for one more. I was playing with a torn labrum mind you. Having one more in me? I didn't think I even had the first four in me. We always have more in us than we think.

It was the fifth game. It should not have come to this, but it did. We were down thirteen to nine in a game that only went to fifteen. All morning long, it had been a constant back and forth rallying of points. A gym that was usually filled with basketball fans had been converted into the high school volleyball championship. The look of defeat was already plastered all over our faces, but the crowd broke into a chant and the words, "I believe that we will win," echoed through the gym. It sparked something in us. We won the point, and the official blew her whistle to signal that I could sub in. I needed to serve five in a row for us to win this game. I was the last person that needed to be behind the serving line, but I was there. I couldn't miss. If I did, the whole vibe in the room was going to change.

One serve. Two serves. Three serves. A couple timeouts were thrown in the mix to try to rattle me, but nothing could shake the confidence that came from hearing our football team scream at the top of their lungs. Four serves.

One more. We only needed one more. My teammates thought it was sweat, but there were tears in my eyes from the pain. I will never forget the moment when I looked up to the stands, and my eyes found my mom. All she did was nod to me. I took it as her saying to me, "You can do this." Later, when I talked to my mom about this moment, she said she remembered me looking at her but had no idea that she nodded her head. Who knows how the Lord created that moment, but I believe that His hand was all over it. The referee signaled for me to serve. I tossed the ball up, took a deep breath, and as loud as it was in the gym I heard nothing until that final whistle blew. Fifteen to thirteen. We had won.

I collapsed to the floor in relief. My whole team dog-piled on top of each other. We shook hands with the other team and circled up with them to pray. The crowd was trying to rush the court, but the officials stopped them. My mom found a way to make her way down to me. She was crying. She took me by the shoulders and told me, "Daddy would be so proud of you." It was too loud in the gym; I didn't hear her verbally say it, but I could read her lips. She pulled me in close so that she could ensure that the next words she said were words that I would hear. "He didn't know that the athlete he wanted so bad for one of his kids to be was going to be you."

We all want the coach. Most of us want it to be our dad. Don't we know that we have a coach, and it has always been our Dad? We have someone who is cheering us on. We have someone who is standing at third base, telling us to keep on running because we are almost home. We have someone telling us that we have what it takes. We have someone telling us that we can do better. We have someone applauding us from the stands. His view is not from the sideline fence; it's from above. We have a coach. He instructs. He guides. He knows the game better than anyone else.

Jesus is so much more than just Lord and Savior. He is everything you think you are lacking. He is everything you want. I wanted a coach. I wanted it to be my dad. He has shown me how all of those things are true of Him. Whatever it is that you need, He can be it. He already is. He has proved this to be true to me, time and time again.

My dad loved Duke basketball. My mom tells the story all the time of when he saw Coach K in the airport and almost passed out. He imparted his love for Duke to my brothers. Years after he passed, I noticed that my oldest brother and my little brother had started a custom of watching the games together. I wanted to join. They refused, as expected. They joked that I was not a real fan. They would quiz me on players' names and ask questions like, "Who did we lose to in 2001 in the NCAA tournament?" I took this as a challenge. I studied Duke basketball. I watched old games online. I was determined to prove myself to them. Slowly they caught on to the fact that I was taking this seriously, and they agreed to let me join. What started as a tactic to get in the room with my brothers turned into an all-in kind of deal.

Over the next couple of years, I started keeping up, and by keeping up, I mean I spent spare time looking up stats and next year recruitments when I should have been paying attention in college. My guy friends always joke that they have never met a girl who knows so much about college basketball (insert emoji of girl with her hand propping up her hair here). It's true.

Game nights at our house have become nights that our weeks are scheduled around. When we don't get to watch the games together, our group text called "Cameron Crazies" goes off the entire game with us acting like little kids on Christmas morning anytime we score a point. The best is when someone's TV is a little ahead of someone else, and we get excited over something they haven't seen yet.

After watching game after game on TV screens, we decided we were going to a game. Both of my brothers would be coming home from school for Christmas break, and it would be the perfect time to road trip to North Carolina. We bought tickets. We booked a hotel. We drove the six hours. We stopped at QT to get the 99 cent slushies. We walked around the campus, decked out in our Duke apparel. We were kids in a candy store.

Right after the game let out we were hanging around, trying to see if we could manage to meet some of the players. My brothers were standing beside each other right outside Cameron Indoor Stadium, the iconic Duke basketball gym. I told them to smile so I could snap a picture. I never wanted to forget this moment.

The next morning, both of them were sound asleep as I turned onto the highway for us to drive home from North Carolina. They didn't know it, but Jesus was teaching me something through all these basketball games. They are the moments that have served as a fill-in where the gaps were created from such heartache of the absence of my dad at all my sports games growing up. No, they aren't father-daughter moments, but they are special moments. I've learned that Jesus has this way of giving us a different type of moments. It's like He shows us that just because we didn't get that one thing doesn't mean He doesn't have something else for you.

That little trip to Duke, every game we have ever sat and watched together, they are the moments I'll remember for the rest of my life. They aren't with my dad, but they are with two people that are spitting images of him. Friends, be encouraged that God has something for you. It might not be what you originally wanted, but with Jesus, nothing He gives will ever disappoint. He might not give you "the" moment, but He will give you some other really special moments. Cherish the moments. All of them. Knowing that each of them are billboard reminders that He never lets us go without. Go Duke!

Days to Come

I wore blue.

My senior year of high school, I convinced my mom to let me take half of my classes online. We all know how online classes go—the only thing that you learn is how to Google answers or how to get around a lockdown browser. Three of my classes were on campus, one of which was guitar. I still laugh about that because I still don't know how to play. I would get to school at 9:00 am and leave at 12:45 pm. It was a dream. I was an athlete, though, so typically I would leave school, drive to my sister's house that was just around the corner, find something to eat in her fridge, take a nap, and then head back to school for practice.

During September of my senior year, we voted for homecoming court. I was not even around because I had already left for the day, but my friends filled me in that it had happened. Honestly, I thought nothing more of it. I was never the girl who campaigned for myself. I really couldn't have cared less. It was my senior year, and I just wanted to be done.

I got a text one afternoon from one of my friends that told me I had made it on to the homecoming court. At that point, a part of me did get the slightest bit giddy inside. I made my way onto Pinterest and picked out the way I would want to wear my hair. I made plans to go dress shopping with my mom and started writing the speech I would have to give in chapel. Every guy and girl on the court that was a senior would give a speech, more so an introduction of who they were so the rest of the school could put a face with the name before everyone voted on who would be king and queen.

Amongst all of this, there was a crucial element of that night that I was letting slip from my memory. The school secretary, that everyone loved, called my name over the intercom while I was sitting in English class. She handed me a form that I would need to fill out for the night. The questions weren't hard. The classic questions they ask a senior, especially a senior at a Christian school.

"How many years have you been here?"

"What is your life verse?"

"What things did you participate in during your time as a student?"

"Where are you intending to go to college?"

All easy to answer, but the fifth question made me recall all the homecoming courts over the years that I had watched from the bleachers.

"Who will you be escorted by?"

As a senior, your dad escorted you that night. They would announce your name over the speakers of the football stadium, followed by, "Escorted tonight by her father ___." I knew that I did not have a name to fill in the blank with. I knew that my valley that David talks about in Psalm 23 was about to be on display for not only my entire school to see but really by my entire town. Some people knew about the passing of my father, but not everyone. This would seal the deal and give everyone an insight into that part of my story.

My mind instantly went into escape mode. I had already decided before I made it back to English class that I was not going to do this anymore. I was terrified for that part of me to be known. I have come to see that it isn't really even the valleys that we are most afraid of, it is people seeing those valleys that we are in. It doesn't feel good when the mask gets peeled off like a Band-Aid in one big rip, and what people see is that you aren't as resilient as they thought. There is a way to avoid this altogether, though. Never put the mask on. Never hide to begin with. Don't walk around declaring your struggles from the rooftops, but let yourself be human and let your humanness show to those around you.

I had fooled everyone in my high school into thinking that I was firm in my faith and firm in the sense that nothing was going to break me. I knew they were about to see otherwise. I hate that I had to learn this lesson this way, but thank God I learned the lesson. I didn't like the curtain being pulled back all of a sudden to reveal my true self, but I saw that I am the only one who can decide whether the curtain stays pulled back or if at times, I let it be drastically drawn like the final scenes of a Broadway musical.

I filled out the form. After wrestling with fear that seemed to be pinning me down on all sides, my hands broke free just enough to answer the final question—my two oldest brothers would escort me. It had never been done before, and it might not ever be done again. For a little while, I wondered what people would think. Would they think I was doing it for attention? Would they think I wanted their sympathy? If only they knew to draw more attention to myself was the last thing I wanted. If they only knew that I did not want their sympathy, I wanted them to treat me like they had treated me before they knew.

Friday night came, and because of my last name, I was the last one to go. I stood at one end of the football field, shaking slightly, but both of my brothers were making jokes to lighten the mood. What stood between me and an entire stadium full of people knowing that my father was absent was twenty yards and an archway that we would walk under. They announced my name, and we walked. We walked across the field, but what I really did was walk straight into my fear, not with bravery but with courage, because courage is doing something despite fear, bravery is doing it without it.

I won homecoming queen that night. They announced my name as the next queen, and my brother threw his hands up in the air with excitement. There is a picture of it that I will cherish forever. I am looking up at him smiling. The crown and sash that are tucked away in my closet say I won something that night, but I won more than just those two relics. The victory wasn't that I did any of this not afraid; the victory was that I did it even though I was. The victory wasn't that I walked across the field, it was that I walked through the valley. I had been playing a game of hide-and-seek, but I never wanted to be found. I had become good at hiding. Jesus wouldn't allow for it anymore. I was using the shadows of the valley as a place to hide, and I believe, for me, He had come into the valley and repetitively said one word: through. "Even though I walk through the valley of the shadow of death, I will fear no evil" (Psalm 23:4).

We can talk about our personal valleys all day long, but we have all been there. The term valley is a universal term that the Lord has given us that each and every single one of us can relate to. I do not have to give a valley a name in order for someone to make a personal connection with it. Pain is pain. A valley is a valley. Often we get so caught up naming the valley that we forget everything else. Sadly, what has started to happen is that we can get obsessed with naming the valleys, and then we start comparing them. I know that Jesus never intended for us to compete with our brokenness. He always intended for us to have compassion for others' brokenness. My friends, why must we keep sharing war stories when we can share battle plans?

I am not belittling identifying where you are at, but I am saying don't think that the end game is to name it. Insecurity, depression, self-hate, etc....Self-awareness will do no good if there is never a tactic to change what you have become aware of. We don't want to just talk about the existence of the valley. We want to talk about what we are going to do when we are in the valley and how to go through it. *Through.* We don't get to stay there. We don't get to take a seat. We don't get to hide. We have to move. We have to walk.

I walked that night. I claimed the victory that was mine to take. It was a milestone for me. However, I knew that it wasn't the only time this would be asked of me. Another time would come. I wore blue that night, royal blue, to be exact. With braided straps going across my back that had tiny studded flowers woven throughout. But one day, one day I will wear white.

One day I will dress in white, stand at the end of an aisle, and stare face to face with my greatest fear since losing my dad—my wedding day. I didn't know how crucial a part dad's played in weddings until I was a part of one only a few short years after his passing. Our family friend's oldest son was getting married. He and his wife had called and asked if I wanted to be a junior bridesmaid. I said yes! I did all the dress shopping, hair fixing, and picture taking. I linked arms with a nine-year-old boy and walked down the aisle. I was out of my dress and into a pair of overalls before the bride could ask me to take any more pictures after the ceremony. My whole family loaded up and headed over to where the reception would take place.

Cocktail hour came, followed by more food and even more food. Then came time for the dance. During the first dance, I stood there giggly as the newly married couple danced their way into the rest of their life. For the mother and son dance, I wanted to be as close as I could because maybe just maybe I could sneak my way in during the song. Then came the father-daughter dance. I didn't know there was such a thing. I was still such a little kid at this time that my brain wasn't even fully registering what was happening and what it meant for me. It wasn't until both of my sisters ran out the back door with my mom chasing after them that the connection started to be made. I followed behind them. My sisters were standing at the bottom of a set of stairs, crying. They weren't speaking words, but their tears were articulating a message to me—we would never get that dance.

From then on out, weddings were things I only attended if it was absolutely necessary. I would always make my way to the bathroom or outside to take a phone call as the father-daughter dance was starting to be cued up. I was in a wedding for a friend a couple of years ago and my escape route wouldn't work. I had to stand up front and watch. The bridesmaids lined the front of the room while the dance took place. Another bridesmaid placed her hand on my back—she knew. Until that moment of the soft touch of another human, I did not even realize that I had not been breathing.

It is a weird feeling. It is a paradox if you may, for the day every girl dreams of, their wedding day, to also be the day you hope never arrives. It is longing for something all the while believing that it could harm you if you get it. I want it to come, but I don't want it to come. I want to walk down the aisle to the man God has planned for me to marry, but I don't want to walk down the aisle without my father on my arm.

How can you want something so bad while at the same time wish it away? This day has not come for me yet. For so long, I never thought I would finish this book until it did. A part of me believed that the Lord would want me to experience that day before I wrote about it. As I sit here now, a 25-year-old, wearing a nightgown from Wal-Mart, marriage is not on the horizon, and honestly, what it has become is an excuse to not finish this book.

"I'll finish it after."

"I don't know what to say to them yet about it because I have not been there."

The conversations I have with myself humor me. I can give myself a pretty good pep talk to not do something. This isn't about me being able to tell you that you can walk down that aisle one day because I did it. It is about me telling myself that I can walk down that aisle one day. People joke that my favorite color is black. Even now, I am seeing the correlation with my fears. Black is the color you tend to wear to a funeral. Black has felt like the only color I would ever get to wear, but it's not true.

One day I will wear white. One day my oldest brother will walk me down the aisle, and my father will not be on my arm or even in the crowd, but he will be and is in my great cloud of witnesses.

One day I'll step to the sound of a song that has rung at times as a nightmare. But the anthem of "here comes the bride" shall never be heard as screeching chalkboard sounds. It is the reminder of the divine union between Christ and the church.

One day I'll meet the man who will not say no to engagement being done the right way just because there is not a father in the picture. He will honor him and honor me by finding another way. He will get creative with it. One day I will stand at the end of the aisle, not just at the start of it tempted to run from it. The aisle will be lined with every man that has taken me in as their own and loved me the way they loved their own daughters. One day, I'll dance. My feet will sway to the sound of my childhood best friend singing the words of Steffany Gretzinger, "You spin me round and round, And remind me of that song, The one You wrote for me, And we dance."[6]

I will dance. Not the way that most do, but I will. I will dance with those same men who lined the aisle. They will be cutting in one at a time, at different times, just as they have over the years. It was always in the way I needed them to and when I needed them to. These men never tried to take a role that wasn't theirs, but they were willing to play an understudy. One day I will get married, and it will be just as much a dream for me as it is any other girl.

I could choose to do away with anything that correlates with the father-daughter idea. I could do away with the dance on my wedding day, but Jesus has not done away with it, so neither will I. It would be easier. I could take measures to protect myself from drawing even more attention to how different my day will look compared to most, or I could maximize on it.

I will let those who have walked this journey with me fill in the gaps as they have done so all these years. I will put the gospel on display by showing that broken pieces are still able to hear the sound of the music. I will dance, fully aware that tears will be streaming down my face. I will dance because I can and because I get to. I will dance because it will be a reminder to every girl in the room that no matter what their relationship with their earthly father looks like, their heavenly Father is beckoning them onto the dance floor.

The promise of heaven is a beautiful thing. All throughout Scripture, we read how the angels sing day in and day out. When I let my childlike imagination run as free as a little girl through a field of dandelions, I imagine that if there is singing in heaven, there is dancing. I can close my eyes and envision it. The throne of grace, surrounded by the melody of His holiness. My dad, cancer-free, his bones not visible like they were the months before he died. No, all I can see now is what I have known all along but so often forget—he is home, right where he wants to be. He is able to dance, taking me by the hand and whispering into my ear, "This dance floor is way better than any one we could have danced on before now."

Maybe he will explain to me that this idea of letting people cut in on the dance is how it was intended to go all along because he will pass me off. He will step back, release his hands from mine, only for his eyes to light up in wonder as he watches my fingers interlock with a new set of hands. These hands have scars. They are much bigger than mine, but they fit like the last piece of a puzzle, undeniable that they are in the right place. They are the hands that cradle the moon and the stars. They are the hands that broke the bread. They are the hands that wiped blood and sweat from a forehead. These hands, they want to hold mine. They want to hold yours. Not just right now, not just in the days that have passed, but for all the days to come.

I'm twenty-five. There is so much life I have yet to face. That is why I chose for this to be the last chapter of the book. My wedding day is a concept of a day to come. There will be more days to come. I wish I could tell you what they will come with. I wish I had all the answers to all the things. Then again, I am glad I don't. It would take away the chance for you to launch an expedition of your own. I have not yet fully arrived and never will until I reach the gates of heaven. I don't want to be a person that looks to someone else to tell me how to do it all. If I don't want to be that kind of person, then I will not allow for myself to be that for someone else. I want you to have to do this on your own some. I want you to discover the gold that can be found if you keep swimming in this cold water. I want you to have your own revelations of who Jesus is.

I am glad that there are days ahead that I haven't figured out. It means there is still room left for me to grow. I am glad there are days like my wedding day or the day I have a child, that I haven't had to face yet. Because as I look back through these pages of recalling the days I have lived through, fifty thousand words prove that the Lord has something for us to learn in all of this.

This was never meant to be an instruction manual of me telling you how to steer this crazy, incredible, out-of-control ship called life. My intentions were never to make the stake in the ground that I am an expert when it comes to living life without a dad. This was supposed to be a letter. A chance for me to let you in a little on my life and what Jesus has done for me. A reminder that everything I thought I lost was found in Jesus.

I sign this final page with gratitude oozing from my fingertips. I sign it with my truest identity. I sign it with the hopes that what will come from this is what always comes from any well-written letter—a response. I don't know what that looks like for you personally, but it's something. I have high hopes that this is just the start of the letter. Add to it for me, send it to someone else. We can never write too much. There are eyes out there looking for words. Yours might just be the ones they are looking for. Your life is a letter. Share it. Send it.

Sincerely,
A little girl

A Great Big Thanks

Mom, you have never wavered in your faith and never once let me believe that anything other than the grace of God enabled you to do what you have done. Thank you for showing me what it looks like to never take any of the credit and for raising me in a home where the gospel was the center. You, above anyone else, have encouraged me to follow Jesus even when everything is falling apart. I hope one day my kids will look up to me in the way I look up to you. Thank you for navigating the role of a single mom with resilience. Thank you for never trying to be what you were not and for living a life that always welcomed us back home.

To my siblings: Anna, Allison, Joseph, Jonathan, and Jacob. You are my home team, and I couldn't have picked a better one. You are the people who taught me what it meant to stand by someone through even the darkest of nights. We have never given up on each other, and I promise that will always be the case. Thank you for not giving up on me. Though our journeys have been different, you have never let me once feel like you would not be there. There is nothing more I could ask for in brothers and sisters. I am better because I have gotten to fight this fight with you. Thank you for letting me share our story.

Mary-Michael, you my faithful friend, could be written into most of these stories as the one who has endured more life with me than anyone else. Words will never be able to adequately express what your role has been in this story of mine. You are the

Samaritan friend. Always meeting me where I am, not needing all the information, never afraid of the mess, and offering what you had. You know what it means to just listen. Thank you for all that you have said, but thank you for all that you haven't. My words have always felt safe with you, written and spoken. Safe is what I needed. I will never stop thanking Jesus that He saw fit for us to be friends. As children we met, but as children I hope we go from here. Until the end, my friend, until the end.

To my other friends: there are so many of you. The ones who I shared this project with long before it ever came out into the public, you believed in this book more than I did at times. You have pushed me and breathed confidence into me when I grew doubtful. You are the unseen heroes behind these pages. You listened when I would call to read parts of it to you. You would be patient when I would tell you I had not touched it in months. You have each challenged my faith and pushed me towards Jesus. I hope one day I get to play the role for you in your dream as you have played in mine.

Lanie-Beth, I long awaited the day the Lord would bring a consistent mentor into my life. I would talk about how much I needed it time after time with friends. You were worth the wait. You have pushed me deeper into the word and further into my calling. No one, and I mean no one, has shown me more generosity in all shapes and forms. Thank you for never being selfish and for always asking, "What can I do for you?" Whether coffee dates, car rides around McDonough or sitting on your couch in your living room, our time is always life-giving. Thank you for being the person I know will answer when I call. I love you LB.

Courtney, heart and soul, my sister. Thank you for trusting me with your children during a time of great grief. Those days in your home healed parts of me. Thank you for letting me share a part of your story. I do not take it lightly. The days behind us are many, but I believe the days ahead are even more. It is an honor to walk with you and your family.

Kevin Marks, Hannah Brencher, Christy Nockels, Katie Jones,

Sydney Smith, and the list could go on and on—to each of you who have leveraged your knowledge, time, and gifts into helping me navigate this book-writing journey.

Dad, our time was cut too short. Though there is much I do not know about you, there has never been a moment where I questioned whether you loved Jesus or not. There is nothing greater a parent can exemplify to their children than that. Thank for you being the man of faith that you were, the kind that people would long talk about after you were gone. I cannot wait until our time comes, and we meet again. There are a lot of conversations we have yet to have. I think eternity is enough time to catch up. Save me a place at the foot of His throne. I cannot wait to worship with you.

My Jesus, a thank You is not adequate for You, but a thank You is all I have to offer. Worthy of all the honor and all the praise, the writer of my story and the writer of this book. I stand speechless at what You have allowed me to be a part of, but more than that, I stand in awe that You would choose me. I am undeserving. Thank You for never letting me go without. Perfect Father, I will gladly take my place as Your child because nothing in this life will satisfy me more than You. Receive these words as an offering. It is not much, but I hand it back over to You. It has always been Yours. Jesus, I love You.

Endnotes

1   C.S. Lewis, *The Last Battle* (New York: HarperCollins, 1956), 228.
2   A.W. Tozer, *The Knowledge of the Holy* (Fig Books, 2012), 4.
3   "Lost Letters," DawnChere Wilkerson, YouTube, accessed November 30, 2019, https://www.youtube.com/watch?v=WQNa6MYtnjc
4   MercyMe, "I Can Only Imagine," *The Worship Project* (1999).
5   "Unfinished Narratives," Adriaking.com, accessed November 30, 2019, http://www.adriaking.com/unfinished-narratives/
6   Amanda Falk and Steffany Dawn Gretzinger, *We Dance* (Bethel Music Publishing, 2014).

CPSIA information can be obtained
at www.ICGtesting.com
Printed in the USA
LVHW092151190220
647590LV00001B/84